Better Homes and Gardens®

C·R·E·A·T·I·V·E
MACHINE STITCHERY

© Copyright 1985 by Meredith Corporation, Des Moines, Iowa.
All Rights Reserved. Printed in the United States of America.
First Edition. Sixth Printing, 1989.
Library of Congress Catalog Card Number: 84-62404
ISBN: 0-696-01435-1 (hard cover)
ISBN: 0-696-01437-8 (trade paperback)

BETTER HOMES AND GARDENS® BOOKS

Editor: Gerald M. Knox
Art Director: Ernest Shelton
Managing Editor: David A. Kirchner

Crafts Editor: Nancy Lindemeyer
Senior Crafts Books Editor: Joan Cravens
Associate Crafts Books Editors: Laura Holtorf Collins,
    Rebecca Jerdee, Sara Jane Treinen
Associate Art Directors: Linda Ford Vermie,
    Neoma Alt West, Randall Yontz
Copy and Production Editors: Marsha Jahns,
    Mary Helen Schiltz, Carl Voss, David A. Walsh
Assistant Art Directors: Harijs Priekulis,
    Tom Wegner, Lynda Haupert
Senior Graphic Designers: Alisann Dixon,
    Lyne Neymeyer
Graphic Designers: Mike Burns, Mike Eagleton,
    Deb Miner, Stan Sams, Darla Whipple-Frain

Vice President, Editorial Director: Doris Eby
Executive Director, Editorial Services: Duane L. Gregg

Senior Vice President, General Manager: Fred Stines
Director of Publishing: Robert B. Nelson
Vice President, Retail Marketing: Jamie Martin
Vice President, Direct Marketing: Arthur Heydendael

Creative Machine Stitchery
Crafts Editor: Rebecca Jerdee
Copy and Production Editor: David Walsh
Graphic Designer: Mike Burns
Electronic Text Processor: Donna Russell

CONTENTS

YOUR MACHINE'S POTENTIAL

♦♦♦

Welcome to the world of machine stitchery, where your imagination will fly and your hands can decorate fabrics spontaneously, precisely, and rapidly. Here you will discover stitchings that illustrate the creative possibilities of machine stitchery as well as a multitude of ways to expand your own machine's versatility and potential.

Before the invention of the sewing machine, a novice seamstress learned her stitches by working samplers. Once she mastered the stitches, she used her favorite ones to embellish whatever was dear to her heart. Nowadays you can do the same thing using your sewing machine.

By stitching small machine samplers such as the pockets on the sewing basket, *left,* you can learn some simple but spectacular techniques, build up your stitching skills, and uncover a variety of ways to use the machine in the future.

On the following pages are projects to make that explore both your machine's and your own creative potential. You'll find appliqué, machine embroidery, couching, smocking, French hand-sewing-by-machine, cutwork, line drawing, and openwork. Complete instructions begin on page 10.

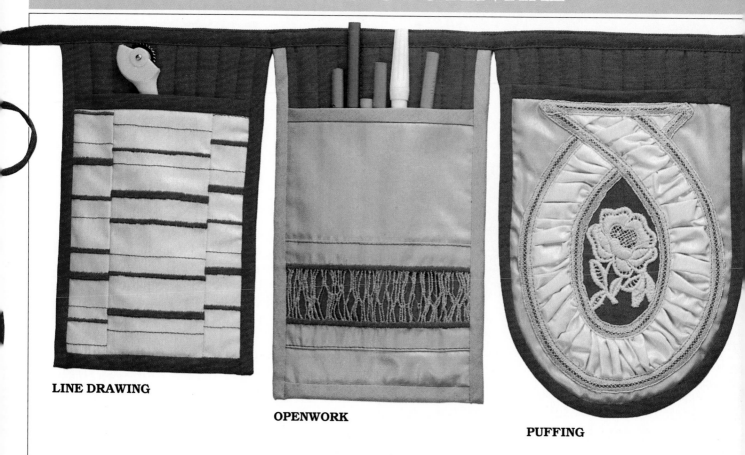

LINE DRAWING

OPENWORK

PUFFING

SEWING SAMPLERS ON YOUR MACHINE

The sampler sewing basket, shown *above* and on page 4, provides the perfect opportunity to explore some techniques without investing much time and money.

Begin by making six 5x8-inch experimental swatches in a variety of materials and stitches. Then, turn the test swatches into handsome, practical pockets to tie around your sewing basket.

To get started, pick an easy sampler. You might combine straight stitching and several widths of satin stitching, as shown in the *Line Drawing* sampler.

Another simple experiment is the *Couching* sampler. Set your machine on loose zigzag settings to fasten thick and thin cordings onto plain fabric. You can add padding behind the fabric swatch for a quilted look.

The *Puffing* sampler explores gathering and combining fabrics, much the same way the *Smocking* swatch does. These stitchings are similar, also, to the construction techniques of *French hand-sewing-by-machine*.

To sample *Openwork*, pull a band of horizontal threads from a piece of woven fabric and zigzag over the

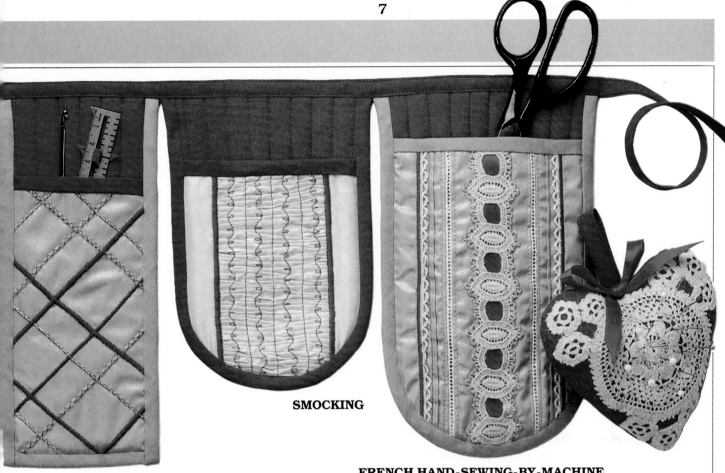

COUCHING

SMOCKING

FRENCH HAND-SEWING-BY-MACHINE

remaining vertical threads. The result is an interesting irregular web of stitches.

When you've finished the samplers, assemble the pockets. Complete instructions begin on page 10.

The infant's shoes, *opposite,* make clever use of *programmed embroidery*—the automatic stitches built into a zigzag machine.

Another type of machine embroidery—*free embroidery*—appears on the English tea cozy, *right.* By varying stitch length and width as the machine runs, you can interrupt programmed stitches to make colorful, irregular stitches. Or, use the straight stitch in free back-and-forth movements to fill in desired areas.

YOUR MACHINE'S POTENTIAL

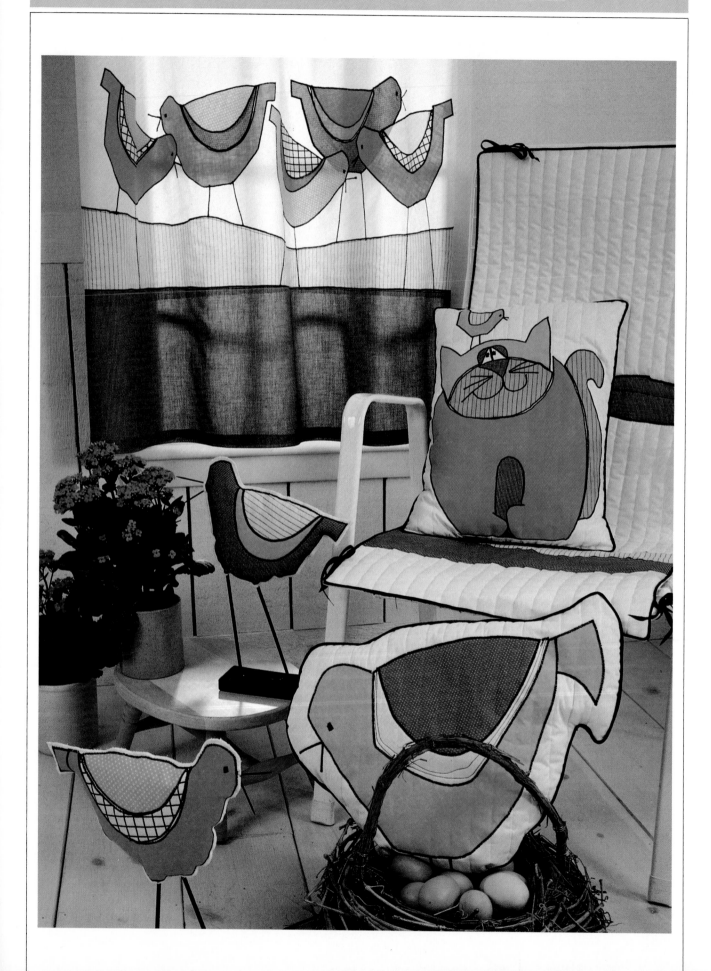

BEGINNER'S APPLIQUÉ AND CUTWORK

The whimsical cat and birds, *opposite,* demonstrate several of the delightful characteristics of machine appliqué.

First, because of the great variety of materials available to contemporary stitchers, machine appliqué is a wonderful vehicle for self-expression. Changing moods is as easy as changing fabrics.

Also, because fabric can be cut into small or large pieces, you can choose between intricate designs and designs that are bold, graphic, and simple. You can take advantage of the precise, clean stitching lines for outlining appliqué shapes.

Best of all, however, machine appliqué works up so quickly you can afford the time to sample all sorts of effects!

Traditional handmade cutwork is treasured for its intricate lacelike appearance.

Contemporary machine cutwork, on the other hand, is admired for its simplicity, clean machine line work, and interesting combination with other sewing techniques.

For your first cutwork sampler, begin with a single, simple, repeated image like the stars on the collar, *above.* Just zigzag around star outlines, cut away the fabric inside the stars, and zigzag over the previous stitching to hide frayed edges.

With that success behind you, move on to cutwork projects like those shown on pages 44–51.

Sewing Basket Samplers

Shown on pages 4–7.

MATERIALS

¼ yard each of ecru, off-white, and cranberry fabrics
½ yard each of muslin and quilt batting
Ecru, off-white, and cranberry sewing thread
Polyester fiberfill
1 khaki, 3 cherry packages of double-fold or wide bias tape
17 inches ¼-inch-wide lace
8½ inches of 1¼-inch-wide lace beading
½ yard ⅜-inch-wide red ribbon
17 inches entredeux
1 yard Belgian lace
Lace doily, flower appliqué
Cording of various thicknesses
Typing paper, marking pen
Elastic sewing thread

INSTRUCTIONS

Line drawing sampler

Cut a 7x12-inch piece of off-white fabric. Working down the long side, zigzag randomly spaced horizontal lines. Vary the line widths and include some single-line stitching. Cut the piece into three vertical strips, one measuring 2¾ inches wide (center strip) and two measuring 2 inches wide (side strips). Turn center panel upside down; join side strips to center with ¼-inch seams.

Openwork sampler

Cut a 5-inch square of loosely woven ecru fabric. Mark a 1¼-inch horizontal band in the center. Pull out a thread at the top and bottom of the band; machine-stitch along these lines. Pull out all horizontal threads between the lines.

Set machine for narrow zigzag; lower feed dogs. Holding the fabric taut and beginning at the bottom, zigzag over several vertical threads at a time. When you reach the top, move to the next several vertical threads and zigzag downward, this time catching the previously worked cord in one or two places. Continue until the band is completed.

Place fabric on a sheet of paper and zigzag with a wide stitch over top and bottom of band; remove paper. Trim upper and lower edges of fabric ¾ inch on either side of band. Turn top and bottom edges under ¼ inch; press. Place band 1 inch from the bottom of a 5x8-inch swatch of ecru fabric; baste. Carefully cut out ecru fabric from behind band area only.

Lay a 2x5-inch piece of red fabric underneath band area; pin and topstitch along fold lines.

Puffing sampler

Refer to photograph on page 6 for pocket design. Draw and cut from paper the shape to be puffed (gathered); pin it to a 5x8-inch ecru swatch and trace around all edges. Remove pattern.

Cut a red center slightly larger than the center of the shape; pin and baste to swatch. Appliqué the flower to the center of the swatch. Zigzag around the red shape.

Cut a 1-inch-wide strip of off-white fabric 45 inches long; gather both long edges. Trace around puffing pattern on another piece of paper; do not cut out. Adjust gathers of strip, pin and baste to paper outline. Straight-stitch, then zigzag along edges.

Pin and baste puffing shape to ecru swatch. Zigzag with red thread several times around edges. Topstitch Belgian lace over the zigzagged edges.

Couching sampler

On a 5x8-inch swatch of ecru fabric, mark diagonal lines. Lay typing paper under swatch and holding cord over the lines, zigzag cord to fabric with red thread. Vary cord thickness and zigzag width, stitching over some lines several times for contrast.

Smocking sampler

On a piece of 4x14-inch off-white fabric, draw a series of horizontal lines ⅜ inch apart across the 14-inch width. With elastic thread in the bobbin and regular thread on the spool, sew along the lines with straight stitches, anchoring ends. Place gathered fabric band on paper; pin. With red sewing thread in the bobbin, embroider over every other line with decorative stitches. Trim band to 3¼ inches long.

French hand-sewing sampler

Center ribbon-threaded lace beading on a 2½x8½-inch ecru swatch. Baste; zigzag edges with ecru thread. On each long edge, stitch entredeux and fabric together with right sides facing. Overcast raw edges. Topstitch on right side. Add a piece of ecru fabric 4⅜x8½ inches to each side of panel, attaching to entredeux.

Mark two tuck lines 1¼ inches from each entredeux on both sides. (Tucks will fold inward toward center.) Fold on first line; baste, then machine-stitch ⅛ inch from edge with red thread. Repeat for opposite side. For second tuck, insert the edge of the lace underneath fold; baste and topstitch. Repeat for other side.

Fabric collage pincushion

Cut front and back of a heart from red fabric, adding ½-inch seam allowance. Appliqué doily to heart center. With right sides facing, sew front to back, leaving an opening for turning. Clip curves, trim seam, and turn. Stuff with fiberfill and sew opening closed. Add bias-tape loop at top for hanging on basket.

Assembling pockets

For padded pocket backs, cut batting, muslin, and red fabric to 9x30 inches. Mark quilting lines every ½ inch across long red strip. Sandwich the batting between the red fabric and muslin; stitch on the lines.

Cut samplers to desired shapes for pocket fronts; cut matching pocket backs from quilted fabric, adding 2–3 inches to tops of backs. Cut a piece of muslin to size of pocket front; lay muslin and front wrong sides together. Cover top edges of pocket fronts with bias tape.

Pin pocket fronts to quilted backs; edge with bias tape. (Do not edge tops of pocket backs.)

To finish

Cut a piece of bias tape 66 inches long. Beginning 18 inches from one end, insert pocket backs into bias tape; baste. Turn in ends; topstitch. Add pincushion after final pocket. Tie pockets to sewing basket and tack tape to basket in several places.

Embroidered Shoes

Shown on pages 5 and 6.

MATERIALS

⅛ yard each of ecru linen and red cotton lining
Red thread, 2 buttons
Water-erasable marking pen
Tissue paper

INSTRUCTIONS

For right shoe, enlarge pattern, *below*, onto paper. Tape pattern to a well-lighted window; tape linen fabric over the design. Trace

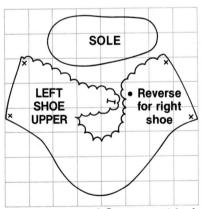

1 Square = 1 Inch

outlines onto the fabric with a marking pen. *For left shoe, flop pattern over and repeat as for right shoe.*

Baste linen to red lining fabric around transfer lines; do not cut out before stitching.

Set zigzag machine for dense scallop motif or similar design and sew along scalloped edges.

Set machine for another decorative stitch and sew ½ inch from scalloped edges and ¾ inch from shoe bottom outlines.

Cut out shoe uppers and soles along outlines, being careful not to cut machine stitches. With right sides facing, match Xs on back seams. Sew seams using ¼-inch allowances. Baste and sew soles in shoe bottoms; turn right side out.

Sew buttonholes at dots on long flaps; sew buttons on remaining dots. To shape shoes, stuff them with tissue paper.

Cottage Tea Cozy

Shown on page 7.

MATERIALS

⅓ yard ocher cotton fabric (roof)
½ yard tan cotton fabric (chimney)
1⅓ yards 45-inch-wide muslin (cottage, lining)
1 yard 45-inch-wide batting
½ yard 25-inch-wide iron-on interfacing
Purple, teal blue, wine red, and blue fabric scraps
10-inch embroidery hoop
Clear presser foot
Assorted sewing threads
Washable transfer marker
Tissue paper

INSTRUCTIONS

Note: ¼-inch seam margins are included in the pattern.

To prepare materials

Enlarge the pattern, page 12, on tissue paper; tape to a well-lighted window.

Cut four 14-inch squares of muslin; place one square face-down in the embroidery hoop. Placing the stretched fabric flat

against the window, trace the design onto the fabric inside the hoop. Use one square for each cottage section, moving the hoop when necessary until all parts are traced. Set pieces aside.

For chimney front, transfer the design to a 14-inch square of tan cotton. Transfer outline of chimney back on tan cotton; cut out. Cut two 1¼x10-inch rectangles for chimney sides, one 1¼x2½-inch rectangle for the top, and one 1¼x3½-inch rectangle for chimney bottom.

For the roof, transfer the stitching, folding, and cutting lines to ocher fabric. Appliquéd pieces for the door, windows, framing, and crossbars are cut from fabric scraps. Add ⅛-inch seam allowances to all edges for turning under. Referring to the enlarged pattern, measure the dimensions of the door and cut from wine-red fabric. Measure and cut the door frame from the blue fabric scrap.

Measure windows and cut from teal blue fabric; cut window frames from purple. Crossbars for the windows and door are cut from ½-inch-wide fabric strips (purple for windows, wine-red for the door). Set all pieces aside.

To embroider

Release pressure regulator; lower feed dogs. Set stitch length to 0; stitch width will be variable, depending upon the area to be embroidered.

Place one of the muslin squares in the embroidery hoop with the drawing on the inside. Turn hoop over so the wrong side of the fabric lies flat on the machine bed; embroidery is done on the drawing inside the hoop.

Turning the hoop as needed, embroider the design colors desired (see photograph for ideas). Stems are made by working horizontally and zigzagging a series of straight lines from left to right along the stem line.

For flowers and leaves, vary the stitch widths according to their shapes. For example, lilacs are made by making a series of small
continued

stitches in groups; heather is sewn similarly, except that the cluster of stitches is done in rows. Omit the vines over the front door; these will be done later.

Complete embroidered designs on all pieces, including the chimney. Do not stitch roof lines.

To appliqué

Refer to pattern for placement of appliqués.

For windows, baste teal blue centers (panes) in place; do not turn edges under. Turn under long edges of crossbars; press and baste over windows; topstitch next to edges with matching thread. Clip inside corners of window frames; turn and press under all edges; baste in place. Stitch next to edges.

Turn under outside edge of door frame; baste in place leaving inside edge raw (door will be placed on top). Machine-stitch along outside edges. Turn and press under raw edges of wine-red door; baste in place; stitch next to edges. Turn under edges of crossbars; baste in place; stitch at edges. Embroider door vines.

To assemble

Note: Before cutting out cottage pieces, redraw the pattern shapes if altered by embroidery; press.

CHIMNEY: With right sides together, sew front to side pieces. Stitch back to sides; turn right side out, press seams. Insert batting cut to same shape as chimney. Turn ¼-inch edges on top and bottom chimney pieces and blindstitch to chimney. Handstitch chimney to cottage in position indicated on pattern.

COTTAGE: With right sides together, sew front of cottage to sides. Sew cottage back to one side only, leaving one to be joined later by hand. Butt lining to correspond to cottage pieces and assemble in the same manner.

Press all seams open. With right sides of lining and embroidered sections facing, sew together along three edges; turn.

Cut batting pieces to correspond to cottage front, back, and sides. Trim off ¼-inch seam allowances and insert batting in appropriate sections, tacking it invisibly in several places. Turn in top and lining seam allowances on open edge of cottage and blindstitch. Join cottage walls together by hand.

ROOF: Cut lining the same size as roof top from tan fabric. Pin roof top and lining right sides together; join, leaving a 4-inch opening. Turn right side out and press edges. Cut batting the same size as roof, minus ¼-inch seam allowances; insert into roof and blindstitch roof closed.

Topstitch thatching design onto each roof section. Fold along top edge and stitch through both sections along the line indicated.

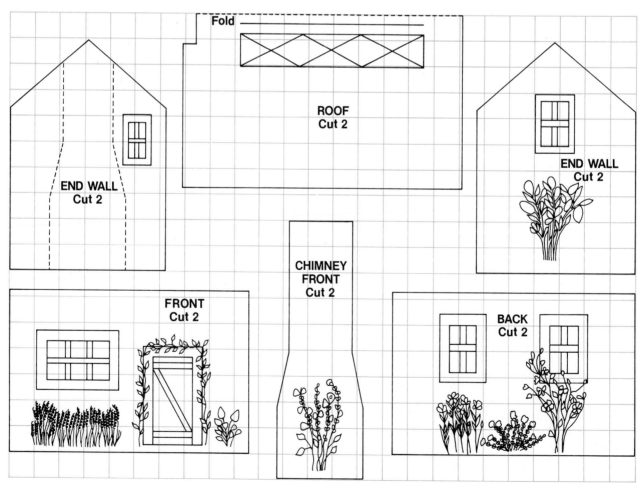

1 Square = 1 Inch

Keeping the cottage square, blindstitch the roof onto the cottage by hand, overlapping the roof about 1 inch on ends and 2 inches on front and back.

Cat and Bird Curtains and Pillows

Shown on page 8.

MATERIALS
1½ yards 45-inch-wide ecru prequilted fabric
1½ yards 45-inch-wide muslin
Ecru curtain panel
1½ yards 18-inch-wide fusible webbing
1 yard 45-inch-wide gray fabric
½ yard each of white pinstripe and gray pinstripe fabric
Gold, yellow, orange, peach, apricot, and salmon fabric scraps
Polyester fiberfill
7½ yards black piping
3 yards ½-inch-wide black ribbon
Black thread
Two ½x9-inch dowels
Toothpicks, pine scraps
Black paint, butcher paper

INSTRUCTIONS
Note: All measurements include ½-inch seam allowances.

For chair pad
Measure quilted fabric to fit your chair (ours is 18x45 inches). Cut pad front; cut matching back from muslin fabric. From gray pinstripe and white pinstripe fabric, cut strips of varied widths (see color photograph on page 8 for approximate size and shape).

With black thread, appliqué strips to pad front, positioning them one-third of the distance from the chair top and one-third of the distance from the bottom.

Sew piping ½ inch from raw edges on pad front. With right sides facing, sew muslin back to front along previous stitch lines, leaving an opening for turning. Turn; press; sew closed. Sew ½-yard ribbon ties to chair pad.

For cat pillow
Enlarge pattern, *below,* onto butcher wrap paper. Cut a 15x21-inch pillow front from prequilted fabric and a matching back from muslin. Cut appliqué pieces from fabric scraps and fusible webbing.

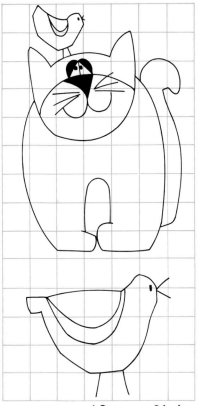

1 Square = 2 Inches

Fuse cat and bird appliqués to pillow front with iron. Machine-appliqué all raw edges with black thread. Add eye, beak, whiskers, and mouth lines with black zigzag satin stitching.

Sew black piping ½ inch from raw edges on pillow front. With right sides facing, sew muslin back to pillow front, sewing along previous stitch line. Leave an opening for turning. Turn pillow right side out; stuff with fiberfill; stitch closed.

For bird pillow
Repeat procedure for cat pillow. Be sure to use a scale of 1 square = 2 inches when enlarging bird pattern.

For bird sculptures
Fuse and machine-appliqué birds to prequilted fabric. Trim excess quilted fabric from appliqué outline, leaving a ¼-inch margin around birds. Appliqué bird edges to muslin rectangles, stuffing birds lightly with fiberfill as you finish the edges. Trim away excess muslin and satin-stitch around bird edges again.

Cut two 9-inch legs from dowels for each bird. Glue legs at ends and insert in bird (it may be necessary to slit a few stitches). Drill holes into 2½x5½-inch pine stand; glue and insert dowel legs in holes. Paint stand and legs black. Insert black-painted toothpicks for beaks.

For curtain panel
Appliqué muslin curtain with a repeated bird design as for the cat pillow. Add a gray fabric strip of varying widths to indicate a landscape. Hem.

Cutwork Star Collar

Shown on page 9.

MATERIALS
Commercial pattern for collar
½ yard each of red, white fabric
Red soutache trim
Red, white thread
Typing paper, marking pen

INSTRUCTIONS
Make a 1¼-inch star pattern. Cut upper collar of white fabric and under collar of red fabric. Stitch a row of soutache trim on upper collar ½ to ¾ inch above seam line. With marking pen, draw stars an equal distance apart, ½ to ¾ inch above the soutache trim.

Place typing paper underneath upper collar and zigzag around the star edges with white thread, pivoting at star points.

Cut out fabric and paper from inside of stars. Zigzag with a slightly wider stitch over previous stitching. Tie off threads. Finish collar according to commercial pattern instructions.

APPLIQUÉ AND EMBROIDERY

♦ ♦ ♦

Embroidery and appliqué are two of the most exciting and versatile decorative techniques to learn on the sewing machine. Besides being less time-consuming than their handworked counterparts, machine techniques give you an opportunity to use unusual materials, to invent as you sew, as well as to add your own personal touches. Here and on the following pages are nine delightful machine projects to introduce you to these two techniques.

"Coffee-time," the appealing design *at left,* is stitched from an interesting, imaginative collection of bits and pieces. Layered atop diminutive wallpaper-like background fabric, the appliquéd pieces are selected for suitable textures and patterns that help to tell the story of the picture.

For example, note the tiny flowered prints used for the dresses, the herringbone wool stove gratings, and the corduroy textures that give structure to the window frames. Even the picture on the wall is fashioned of flowers cut from a scrap.

With attention to the last detail of the beads for buttons and lace trims, the creator of "Coffee-time" makes effective use of her fabric in describing the scene.

To learn the art of appliqué, begin with "Coffee-time" or a design of your own based on an old family photograph. Sort through your precious bits and pieces of fabric saved from previous projects, checking for materials to use in making a picture. Then turn the page for basics on how to appliqué on your machine. Complete instructions begin on page 23.

PATCHWORK PICTURE MAKING

Once you've chosen a design for your patchwork picture and supplied yourself with more fabric than you really need, the fun can begin. Make a simple outline drawing to follow as you freehandedly cut the composition parts, *top.*

Or, if you prefer to pin paper patterns to fabric for a careful cutting of the original drawing, use the drawing as a plan and make an actual-size drawing to cut apart into pattern pieces.

Cut all pieces from fabrics, selecting textures and prints that suit the parts of the picture. Then, working from the background toward the foreground, carefully pin and baste them in place on a padded background fabric, *center.*

With a zigzag sewing machine set for medium-wide, closely spaced satin stitches, sew over all the raw edges, leaving a smooth, defined line around each shape, *bottom.*

Selecting the right thread is every bit as important as selecting the right fabric for a design; matching threads become an integral part of the shapes while contrasting threads outline them clearly.

COUNTRY SCENES

The simple images of these rural scenes translate easily into machine embroidery once you've painted the background shapes. Just freely embroider the painted areas with a variety of stitches to make tiny flowers, rolling hills, and bright blue skies.

Before you begin to embroider the design on the machine, draw the design on muslin. Paint the shapes with flat (unshaded) colors of fabric paint, as shown *at right*. The colors enhance the sewing thread applied over them, keeping the thin threads looking firmly set into the composition.

When the fabric is dry, it can go into the machine, *far right*. With plain, straight stitches and bits of quilt batting behind some areas for padding, quilt parts of the picture, outlining some of the shapes. Then, texture other areas with straight stitches worked back and forth until the shapes are filled.

TWO WAYS TO 'HOOK' A RUG

Yes, you can "hook" a rug on your sewing machine, and not just one way, but two! Once you've mastered the techniques for hooking the two rugs on these pages, you can apply what you've learned to sewing other embroidered objects like the crewel-look pillows, *above left*.

The white and yellow rya look-alike rug on this page is made by wrapping rug yarn around a hairpin lace frame, then stitching down the frame's center with nylon thread to form long yarn strips.

To put the rug together, position the strips of looped yarn on a fabric backing and stitch them down the center a second time, as shown *at right*. Then either cut the yarn for a shaggy look or leave the loops uncut.

Another inventive way to hook a rug on the machine is by attaching yarn loops to a fabric background one loop at a time. The yarn loops of this splashy oval rug are placed close together and the surface is stitched outward from the center of the decorative motifs.

To get started, choose a sturdy woven fabric—such as burlap or painter's canvas—and define the stitching areas by drawing the design on the surface with a marker.

Remove the presser foot and replace the spool with clear nylon thread. Beginning with a floral area, stitch the yarn end to the backing. Next, pull up a yarn loop to the right of the needle and stitch over the base of the loop, *right.* Continue stitching loops, filling in the shape and changing colors as needed (see *far right*). .

APPLIQUE AND EMBROIDERY

DESIGNING FABRIC WITH FANCY STITCHES

I f your sewing machine has more decorative stitches or cams than you could shake a needle at, don't ignore them—use them creatively to turn out unique fabrics designs.

To become your own fabric designer, choose a durable, medium-weight cotton, preshrink it, pick a stitch setting, and sew up a bolt of fabric with a selection of your machine's decorative stitches. Then sew the fabric into practical items like the pillows, tablecloth, and daybed cover shown here.

With that successfully accomplished, the sky's the limit! You can invent hundreds of ways to design fabrics to decorate your home, your children's clothing, or gifts you'll be proud to give away.

BEAUTIFUL BARGELLO ON CANVAS

You can duplicate the delicate look of traditional handworked needlepoint in a fraction of the time on your zigzag sewing machine. All you need to "needlepoint" are vibrant colors of sewing thread and 18-mesh needlepoint canvas, as shown *at bottom right*.

To begin your bargello needlepoint, guide the needle into the first mesh. Letting the needle swing back and forth across the open mesh, allow the threads to build up on the surface, as shown *top right*. Then, positioning the needle in the next row *and* two meshes away from the first set of stitches, follow the pattern to the row's end. Change thread colors for the next rows *(center)*.

Coffee-time Appliqué

Shown on pages 14–15.

Finished size is 14x17 inches.

MATERIALS
17x20 inches each of
   background fabric and
   prequilted muslin
Assorted solid and print fabric
   scraps (see suggestions *below*)
Sewing threads in a variety of
   color choices
9 pearl beads for dresses
2 small black beads for stove
Small silver bead (coffeepot lid)
Lace scraps
Paper, tracing paper
14x17-inch wooden artist's
   stretcher strips

INSTRUCTIONS

Fabric suggestions
Careful and creative selection of appropriate fabrics will enhance the three-dimensional quality of this machine-appliquéd picture. Developing a color scheme is easier once you've chosen the major fabric, so begin with the background fabric. Consider a wide variety of textures, patterns, and colors, evaluating each fabric by itself and in combination with others.

To achieve a design similar to the one shown, choose a small print for the wallpaper, a floral print for the picture frame, a blue-and-gray print for the "enamel" coffeepot, combinations of black-and-gray prints and solids for the stove, faded light blue denim for the sky, and assorted compatible fabrics for the other areas.

To begin
Make a master pattern by enlarging the diagram, *right*, onto plain paper. Trace the enlarged design onto tracing paper for a working pattern. Cut the working pattern apart and pin the pieces to appropriate fabrics; cut out fabric appliqués without adding seam allowances.

Baste the prequilted backing to background fabric with muslin side facing away from the background fabric.

Pin and baste pattern pieces to background fabric, referring to the master pattern for placement. For basting, use contrasting threads that are easy to see. Lightweight fabrics may need to be lined with iron-on interfacing for added support.

To machine-appliqué
Setting your machine for a medium-wide, close satin stitch, sew over all raw edges of each appliqué. For best results, use even hand tension on the fabric; guide, do not push or pull, the fabric.

When the design requires stitching a sharp corner, stitch up to the corner; lower the needle into the fabric at the outside of the line of stitches. Then lift the presser foot and pivot the fabric. Lower the presser foot and continue stitching.

If your machine has a variety of decorative stitch settings, you may wish to embellish the design with fancy stitching in matching or contrasting colors of thread.

Once machine-appliqué is completed, pull sewing threads to the back and trim. Remove all basting stitches.

Embroider facial features by hand using one strand of sewing thread or a single strand of embroidery floss; add beads and lace trims in appropriate places.

To finish
Steam-press the finished piece lightly on the wrong side of the fabric. Assemble artist's stretcher strips into frame.

Center frame on appliqué and mark corners with pencil. Stand frame on longest side; center one long edge of appliquéd picture on frame edge and staple at center. Pull the right corner of picture slightly past its mark and staple. Repeat at the opposite corner. Fill in the frame edge with staples, working from center toward corners and pulling the fabric taut to avoid puckers.

Staple opposite edge of the picture using same procedure, working from center toward corners. Repeat for short sides.

For corners, trim excess fabric from underside, leaving background fabric uncut. Fold into mitered corners and staple.

1 Square = 1 Inch

Embroidered Ducks

Shown on page 17.

Finished size for picture is 13½x13¾ inches.

MATERIALS
15-inch muslin or cotton square
10- or 12-inch-diameter
  embroidery hoop
5½-inch muslin square (facing)
5½-inch square of quilt batting
⅛ yard of cotton print (framing)
Assorted sewing threads
Acrylic paints
2 pieces mat board, each
  13¾x13¼ inches
Transparent tape, fabric glue

INSTRUCTIONS
Enlarge the design, *right*, on paper and tape it to a well-lighted window. Center and tape the 15-inch square of muslin over the design and trace it lightly onto the fabric with a pencil.

To paint fabric
Place the fabric on several layers of paper towels. Mix paint with enough water to give it a creamy consistency. Dip a small brush in paint and remove excess water by lightly dabbing the brush on a paper towel. (Excess water will make the paint bleed onto the fabric.) Do not overload brush with paint.

Beginning with large areas first, paint *up to but not over* outlines. To prevent colors from bleeding, make sure each painted area is dry before beginning an adjacent area. Refer to photograph for placement of colors to complete painting.

To embroider design
Sandwich the quilt batting between the design and the 5½-inch square of muslin; baste in place. Release the pressure regulator, lower the feed dogs on your machine and stretch the basted fabric inside an embroidery hoop.

Using straight stitches and white thread, sew around outside of ducks and wings. With orange thread, stitch outline of feet and beaks. Machine-embroider sky by

1 Square = 1 Inch

stitching horizontal blue lines fairly close together. Move embroidery hoop as needed.

Machine-stitch flowers, making various sizes and shapes in orange, yellow, and white thread.

For grass, fill in background freely with bright green vertical stitches. Overstitch the shadows with dark green thread. To finish, make black French knots by hand for the eyes.

To finish
Remove stitchery from hoop. Using a ruler, mark picture front with pencil to measure 6⅞x6½ inches. Trim, allowing a ⅝-inch seam allowance around marked square.

Cut cotton print into two 7¾x4-inch strips and two 16x4-inch strips. Pin short strips to top and bottom of picture, right sides facing; stitch. Press open. Pin long strips to picture sides and sew; press open.

Center and stretch picture over one mat board. (Trim the board, if necessary, to allow for ample overlap.) Attach to back side on board only, using a fabric glue.

Trim second piece of mat board slightly smaller; coat entirely with glue and adhere to back of picture. Add hanging attachment.

Kentucky Barn Soft Box

Shown on page 17.

Finished size for box is 7x6¼x4 inches.

MATERIALS
15-inch square muslin or cotton
10- or 12-inch embroidery hoop
Scrap muslin 2½x7 inches
Three 2-inch muslin squares
  (facing)
½ yard of quilt batting
½ yard of cotton print for box
15x20-inch mat board for box
Acrylic paints
Assorted sewing threads
Transparent tape, pencil, ruler

INSTRUCTIONS

To transfer the design and to paint the fabric, refer to instructions for Embroidered Ducks, page 24. For placement of colors, see photograph on page 17.

To embroider design

Lower the feed dogs. Place a piece of batting 2½x7 inches, followed by the same-sized muslin scrap, behind barn and clouds (wrong side); baste. Stretch in embroidery hoop.

With straight stitches, outline barn roof, barn, barn doors, and cloud shapes, using thread that is color coordinated. Trim excess batting. To embroider sky, straight-stitch with blue thread in closely spaced horizontal lines. Move embroidery hoop as needed.

For fields, place batting and muslin behind several sections of the design and straight stitch in rows ¼ inch apart, using matching thread. Trim excess batting. Make ¼-inch-wide rows of dense, wide zigzag stitching on two sections. For remaining sections, fill in freely with closely spaced vertical stitches. Refer to how-to photographs on page 17.

Remove embroidered picture from hoop. Center design within a rectangle measuring 7 inches (top, bottom edges) by 6¼ inches (sides). Mark edges, then cut on marked lines (seam allowance is included).

To make soft box

Cut cotton print box fabric as follows:
   3 pieces, 7x6¼ inches (top, bottom of box)
   4 pieces, 4½x6¼ inches (sides)
   2 pieces, 14x7 inches (back, bottom, front)
   Cut mat board as follows:
   2 pieces, 6x3½ inches (front, back of box)
   2 pieces, 5x3½ inches (sides)
   2 pieces, 6x5 inches (top and bottom of box)

Beginning with top section, pin embroidered picture and cotton print, right sides together. Stitch a ¼-inch seam around three edges, leaving top edge open; turn. Wrap a layer of batting around a 6x5-inch mat board; insert into opening. Turn ¼ inch on open edges to inside and slip-stitch closed.

For side, pin two pieces of cotton print fabric (4½x6¼ inches), right sides together. Stitch a ¼-inch seam around three edges, leaving one edge open; turn. Wrap batting around a 5x3½-inch mat board and insert into pocket; slip-stitch closed, turning in ¼ inch. Repeat for other side.

Pin the two 14x7-inch pieces, right sides together (this includes back, bottom, and front of box); stitch a ¼-inch seam along three edges, leaving one long 14-inch edge open. Turn.

With ruler, measure and mark a line 4¼ inches across from top of long strip (back of box). Mark another line 5½ inches below (bottom of box). The remaining 4¼-inch section is the front.

Wrap batting as before around the three mat boards for these sections (two pieces 6x3½ inches, one piece 6x5 inches). Insert all three boards into appropriate sections of the pocket. Fold open edges ¼ inch to inside and slip-stitch. Machine-stitch along marked lines.

Fold back and front sections up. Blindstitch sides to front, back and bottom edges. Tack top to box at back edge.

Rectangular Rug

Shown on page 18.

Finished size is 3x5 feet.

MATERIALS
Four 2-ounce skeins of rug yarn
   (4 white, 4 yellow)
2½-inch and 4-inch hairpin lace
   frames
Clear nylon thread for spool
White thread for bobbin
1¾ yards duck canvas or burlap
Liquid latex rug backing
Tissue paper

continued

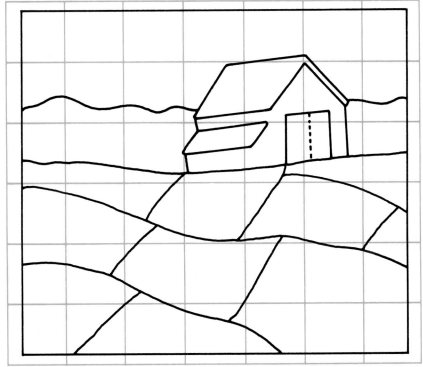

1 Square = 1 Inch

APPLIQUÉ AND EMBROIDERY

INSTRUCTIONS

To prepare materials

Cut a 40x64-inch piece of rug backing. Draw a line 2 inches from all raw edges to define margins around the rug.

To make white rug yarn loops, use the 2½-inch lace frame. With the curved part close to you, begin wrapping yarn around the frame, keeping the loops close together.

Lower the feed dogs on the machine. After several inches of loops have been wrapped, stitch down through the middle of the lace frame, using nylon thread on the spool and white in the bobbin. Keep yarn loops close together, avoiding gaps.

As the yarn is stitched, let it slide off the open end of the frame. Pull the frame toward you and continue wrapping and sewing until you've made a strip 50½ inches long. Wrap and stitch at least 17 additional strips. Set aside for rug construction.

Prepare yellow strips in the same manner, using the 4-inch lace frame for wrapping. Make eight 36-inch and eight 50½-inch strips. Set aside.

To stitch rug

Place a large piece of tissue paper or lightweight interfacing under the piece of rug canvas to prevent puckering.

For yellow border, center a yellow strip on the 2-inch line along rug end. Using nylon thread on the spool and white in the bobbin, stitch down the center of the yarn strip over previous stitching to secure it to the backing.

Fold loops over and begin the second full row of yellow by placing the center seam of the new strip ¼ inch from the stitching line of the first row toward rug center. Continue for three rows.

Repeat for the other rug end; then sew four rows to each side, completing the area within the end borders of the rug.

Fold final row of yellow loops over on long edge and stitch a strip of white in the same manner as before. Continue attaching strips at ¼-inch intervals until center area is filled. Make additional strips as needed.

To finish rug

Clip the yellow yarn loops; do not cut the white.

Turn the 2-inch margin to the rug back and press; slip-stitch in place. Apply a nonskid backing of liquid latex, if desired.

Note: The rug is sturdy but not designed for high-traffic areas.

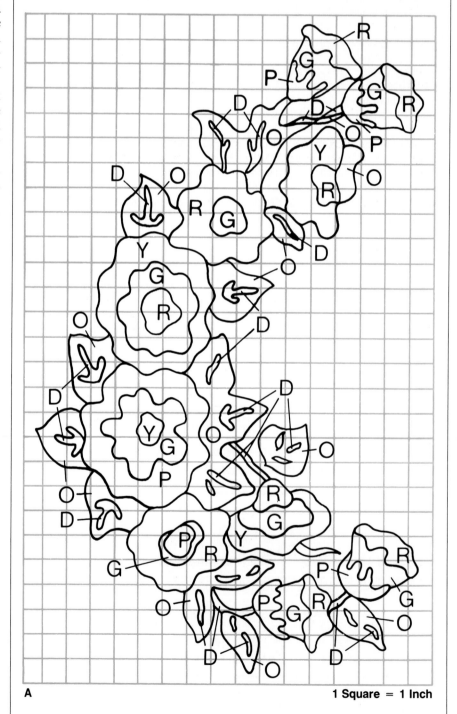

A   1 Square = 1 Inch

Oval Rug

Shown on page 19.

Finished size is 26x44 inches.

MATERIALS
1⅛ yards washable duck canvas
   or rug burlap (backing)
Three 2-ounce skeins of ivory or
   white rug yarn
½ skein of rug yarn in each of
   the following colors: yellow,
   gold, rust, plum, olive green,
   and dark green
Knitting needle
Tissue paper
Clear nylon thread for spool
White thread for bobbin
Dressmaker's carbon paper
Liquid latex rug backing

INSTRUCTIONS
   Enlarge patterns A and B,
pages 26 and 27, on paper. Using
dressmaker's carbon paper,
transfer design to a 28x46-inch
oval of backing fabric. Follow oval

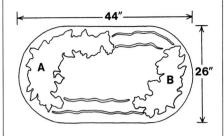

drawing, *above,* for proper placement of rug motifs.
   Place a large sheet of tissue paper under the fabric backing to
help prevent puckering while
stitching the rug.
   Remove machine presser foot
and lower feed dogs. Beginning
with the design areas and following the color key, *below,* stitch
loops of yarn to canvas backing.

Color key:
D - Dark green
O - Olive green
P - Plum
G - Gold
R - Rust
Y - Yellow

To attach yarn loops to the
backing, first stitch the end of a
length of yarn to the material. Using the knitting needle to the
right of the sewing needle, pull up
a yarn loop. Stitch over the base
of the yarn loop to secure it to the
backing. Continue pulling and
stitching loops in this manner to
complete each color area.
   To fill in the ivory background
areas faster, use several lengths
of yarn together and pull up more
than one loop at a time; then
stitch across all loop bases at the
same time.
   When rug is completed, turn
the 2-inch fabric margin to the
back of the rug and press. Slip-
stitch margin in place, trimming
excess to eliminate bulk. Apply a
nonskid backing of liquid latex, if
desired.
   Note: The rug is sturdy but not
designed for high-traffic areas.

Embroidered Fabric

Projects using this technique are
shown on pages 20–21; see specific projects on pages 27–29.

MATERIALS
Sewing machine with decorative
   stitch settings or cams
Cotton or cotton-blend fabric
White, blue, green, and black
   thread
Yardstick
Tailor's chalk or transfer pen

INSTRUCTIONS
   Preshrink fabric. Choose any
two compatible decorative stitch
settings for the design. One stitch
setting is used for the outer rows
and a second stitch for the center.
   Placement of rows may be mea-
sured and marked on the fabric,
using a yardstick and tailor's
chalk. (A quilter attachment may
be used to keep rows straight and
evenly spaced.)

continued

B   1 Square = 1 Inch

After selecting project and marking stitching lines, place white thread in the bobbin and a colored thread on the spool. Stitch all rows of one color in one decorative stitch. Switch to the second decorative stitch and add parallel rows in a second or third color choice.

Daybed Cover

Shown on page 20–21.

Finished size is 30x72 inches.

MATERIALS
10 yards of machine-embroidered fabric, 44 inches wide
17½ yards of cable cord
4½ yards muslin
2 yards heavy-duty snap tape
Thread, yardstick
Transfer pen or tailor's chalk

INSTRUCTIONS
Note: This cover can be made to fit any size mattress. Instructions include general how-to with dimensions for pictured daybed given in parentheses.

To prepare materials
Take bed measurements as follows: mattress top (30x72 inches); mattress side or boxing strip (4x204 inches); height of box spring from floor (15 inches); mattress circumference (204 inches plus 12 inches for waste).

If cording is desired on top and bottom mattress edges and on skirt top, measure entire circumference of mattress and multiply that amount by 3 (612 inches). Divide this number by 36 to convert to yards (17 yards plus ½ yard for seams).

Preshrink cable cord, fabric, and snap tape.

To embroider fabric
Refer to Embroidered Fabric instructions on page 27 for general embroidery how-to.

The daybed fabric design is formed from five horizontal and nine vertical rows of stitching, using two stitch settings.

For the vertical pattern, a black center stitch is bordered by four alternating blue and green rows on each side. The horizontal pattern consists of only five rows: a black center bordered by two blue and green rows.

To sew daybed cover
Cut a piece of embroidered fabric the width and length of the mattress top, adding ½-inch seam allowances. If the strip is to match the design of the mattress top, add extra length to the strip, piecing it together if necessary.

Cover enough cord for top and bottom of mattress edges. Machine-baste cord and raw edges together to both sides of the boxing strip along seam line. Matching design lines, stitch the boxing strip to the top piece with right sides together.

Cut a muslin piece the dimensions of the mattress top for the underside of the daybed mattress. Stitch muslin, right sides facing, to the boxing strip along three sides, leaving one long side open. To both the muslin base and the boxing strip, sew snap tape along the opening. Clip corners, grade seams, turn, and press.

To make an inverted box-pleated skirt, add 3 inches to the height of the box spring (18 inches). Cut the embroidered fabric to this width. The yardage needed for the inverted pleated skirt is equal to twice the circumference of the box spring (408 inches). Piece the strip together, if needed; add ½-inch seam allowances to the strip ends.

Hem the skirt strip before the ends are joined, turning under ½ inch. Turn under 2 inches and stitch.

To mark pleats, place the fabric strip on the floor. Starting 3 inches from the raw edge at one end, place pins every 6 inches along the full length of the fabric to indicate pleat fold lines. The final pleat mark should be 3½ inches from the fabric end.

Starting at the second pin, make inverted box pleats every 6 inches along the length of the fabric by bringing one fold line to the next. Pin pleats in place and press.

Stitch skirt ends together; make the final pleat over this seam. Cover sufficient cord for the skirt top; stitch it in place along the seam line.

Adding ½-inch seam allowances, cut a muslin piece equal to the dimensions of the box spring top. Sew, right sides facing, to the top of the daybed skirt to complete the cover.

Tablecloths

Shown on page 20.

Finished size for square cloth is 44 inches. Circular cloth is 96 inches in diameter.

MATERIALS
1¼ yards machine-embroidered fabric for square cloth
5⅓ yards 54-inch-wide print fabric for circular tablecloth
Thread, yardstick
Transfer pen or tailor's chalk

INSTRUCTIONS

Square tablecloth
For general embroidery how-to, refer to Embroidered Fabric instructions on page 27.

To embroider the even diagonal design for the square tablecloth, begin a row in one corner of the fabric, working out to either side of the pattern. Make diagonal rows of three lines each: Black is stitched in the center and bordered on each side with a second decorative stitch.

To finish the embroidered cloth, turn under the raw edge ¼ inch and press. Turn the pressed edge under ¼ inch and baste. Press the hem and blindstitch.

Circular tablecloth

Measure the diameter of the tabletop and add the number of inches of drop to either side. Table shown on page 20 is 36 inches in diameter with a 30-inch drop on each side, totaling 96 inches. Add a ½-inch hem allowance all around.

Use one width of the fabric for the center of the table and split remaining widths on each side to make a 106-inch square. Using ½-inch seams, stitch the three strips together with patterns matching. Press seams open.

Fold fabric in quarters. Tie string to a pencil; cut string to 48 inches. Use a thumbtack to hold the end of the string in place at the folded corner of the fabric. Holding the pencil at the free end of string, draw a quarter-circle arc. Add a ½-inch seam allowance to the arc; cut through all four fabric layers.

Turn raw edges under ¼ inch. Fold up ¼ inch and hem.

Ruffled Pillow

Shown on page 21.

Finished size is 12 inches square.

MATERIALS
½ yard 44-inch-wide machine-embroidered fabric
1 yard of contrasting fabric for pillow ruffle
Polyester fiberfill
Thread, yardstick
Transfer pen or tailor's chalk

INSTRUCTIONS

Cut two 14-inch squares of fabric for pillow front and back. For the ruffle, cut enough 8-inch-wide strips of contrasting fabric to form one 4-yard strip of fabric. Sew the strips together, using ¼-inch seams.

To embroider fabric

Refer to Embroidered Fabric instructions on page 27 for general embroidery how-to.

Make diagonal rows of three lines each: Black is stitched in the center and bordered by one blue alternate decorative stitch on each side.

To stitch pillow

Fold fabric strip in half lengthwise, wrong sides facing; press. Machine-baste raw edges together. Gather strip by hand or by machine. With right sides facing, baste and pin raw edges of ruffle to pillow front. Tucking ruffle inside, pin and stitch pillow back to front. Leave one side open for turning. Clip corners, turn, and press. Stuff pillow; slip-stitch opening closed.

Bargello Chair Seat

Shown on pages 21 and 22.

MATERIALS
Zigzag sewing machine
22-inch square (or size to fit chair seat) each of 18-mesh mono needlepoint canvas and polyester batting
White, purple, dark blue, light blue, olive green, yellow, and gold sewing threads
Board for seat backing
Masking tape
Waterproof marker
Staple gun and staples
Soil retardant spray

INSTRUCTIONS

Cover the canvas edges with masking tape to prevent raveling. With a waterproof marker, draw the outline of the chair seat on the canvas. Extend pattern at least ½ inch beyond these borders to allow sufficient stitched canvas to overlap to back of seat.

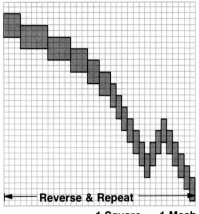

Reverse & Repeat
1 Square = 1 Mesh

To embroider chair seat

Place purple thread on the spool and white in the bobbin. Referring to the diagram, *above, right,* as a stitch guide, count canvas mesh so peak of bargello design falls along the border of the needlepoint canvas.

Set machine for a wide zigzag stitch. Lower feed dogs and remove presser foot. Beginning at the widest end of the canvas, place the needle into the first mesh. Pull up on the needle, bringing the bobbin thread to the top of the canvas to prevent threads from jamming.

Place the needle into the fourth mesh (follow diagram for proper placement). Bar-tack across these 4 meshes to allow threads to build upon the canvas surface (approximately 5 times).

Place your needle in the next row, two meshes above the first set of bar tacks. Continue placing your needle and bar-tacking in this manner, finishing the row.

For the second row, change the top spool to dark blue thread. The order of colors to complete the pattern is purple, dark blue, light blue, olive green, yellow, and gold.

To finish

Cut the chair backing board to fit chair seat dimensions exactly. Sandwich a layer of polyester batting between the backing board and the completed canvas.

Turn all three layers over and secure the canvas to the backing board with a staple gun or tacks. Clip corners wherever necessary.

TREATS FOR CHILDREN

♦ ♦ ♦

Every child loves a party, a treat,
or just a day to celebrate being a kid.
For you, half the fun is in the
anticipation while you prepare the
things that make those special days
memorable. Here and on the following
pages you'll find 11 easy-to-sew
designs full of whimsy, color,
and imagination. Best of all, they're
sure to please the kids.

For knockout birthday celebrations, the appliquéd tablecloth, *left,* adds color and zest to one birthday after another. The lacy cake slices are ever-fresh and the candles always lit— just ask your child to pick the number that suits her age!

When your partygoers are looking for something spectacular to wear, surprise them with ordinary dresses bedazzled with buttons and machine buttonholes. For kids who prefer blue denims, spruce up their pants with embroidered knee patches, *left.*

And there's lots more. For quick ways to personalize a layette, make lovable dolls, and splash color on children's clothing, please turn the pages. Complete instructions begin on page 38.

LITTLE GIRLS' FANCIES

Adding a hand-crafted name is often all it takes to turn a ho-hum item into the perfect gift for someone special. And it's so easily done when you use your personal handwriting.

To personalize infant clothing like the examples, *above,* use a water-soluble transfer pen. Write the baby's name in a prominent place on a hand-stitched or ready-made garment.

Then, with your machine threaded in contrasting thread and set for satin stitches, sew over the lines.

Any proud new mom would be thrilled with your thoughtful gift!

Some occasions are just perfect for an out-and-out display of sweet sentimentality—and what could be sweeter or more sentimental than the huggable Victorian dolly-with-a-doll *at right?*

If you really want to sew to the limits—make your own little doll a dress to match her dolls, embellishing it with a richly machine-embroidered crazy-patch vest, *right.*

TREATS FOR CHILDREN

FOR PLAY AND SLEEP: A PALETTE OF COLORS

Any ordinary day becomes a celebration when you sew with color. And the kids will love the colors, too.

With a flick of the wrist you can splash appliquéd color on a painting shirt, *opposite,* to make someone feel like an artist. Just be sure you have a variety of thread colors and fabric scraps to do a great job.

For more fun, as well as a little teaching, appliqué the names of colors on preschoolers' clothing. You'll need small amounts of fabric in basic colors and plenty of matching threads.

If bright machine embroidery is your cup of tea, you can lavish color all over a youngster's linen. The lettering on the sheet and pillowcase, *above,* was made with one row of satin stitches around each letter.

Colors were interchanged in a free-wheeling fashion, although they were planned ahead to avoid too many thread changes.

To get started on your own linens, purchase large letter or stencil sets. Or enlarge small letter sets to desired size. If widths on the letters are wider than your widest satin-stitch, sew parallel stitching rows to achieve the proper width.

TREATS FOR CHILDREN

PLAYTIME PINUPS FOR A CHILD'S ROOM

Kids' young-at-art sense of color, line, and perspective has a freshness and originality that translates easily into appliqué. The child-designed basketball players, *far left,* make lively additions to a youngster's room.

Just cut basic shapes from fabric, fuse them onto background material, and appliqué. Then back them with felt, stuff lightly, and pin them up.

Another quick pinup is the easy-appliqué brag jacket that sports the room occupant's award collection, *left.*

Embellish a ready-made jacket with patches and memorabilia from school, scouts, and summer camp. Or decorate the jacket with logos and emblems that show the child's preference for cars or baseball teams.

Birthday Tablecloth

Shown on page 30.

Finished size is 44 inches square.

MATERIALS
Hemmed 44-inch square of blue dotted fabric
Appliqué scraps
Matching threads
⅔ yard of 1-inch-wide lace
Number stencils
Fusible webbing
Paper, transfer pen

INSTRUCTIONS
Enlarge the pattern, *below*, onto paper. Cut apart the individual pattern shapes, pin them to fabric scraps and fusible webbing, and cut out. For the cake plates, cut lace pieces to fit around the slices.

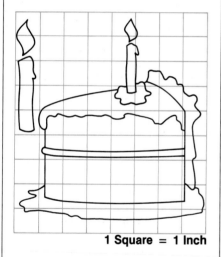

1 Square = 1 Inch

With a transfer pen, trace numbers onto assorted fabrics; cut them from fabric and fusible webbing. Fuse the cake slices, numbers, and candles in a random design on the tablecloth. Set your machine for a close, medium-wide zigzag stitch and satin-stitch around all raw edges with matching threads.

Full-size

Sheep Knee Patch

Shown on page 31.

MATERIALS
Child's jeans
5-inch-square blue denim patch with rounded corners
White, green denim scraps
Light blue, black, white, green, royal blue, and red thread
Water-soluble transfer pen, fabric glue, and tracing paper

INSTRUCTIONS
Trace the full-size pattern, *above*, onto tracing paper. Cut the sheep's body from white denim and the ground from green.

Glue sheep and ground to blue patch. With the transfer pen, draw in areas to be embroidered.

To embroider, release the pressure regulator and lower the feed dogs on your machine. Loosen the bobbin tension and set the stitch length to 0. With black thread, zigzag over the head, ears, and legs of the sheep, varying the stitch width as needed to fill in the areas.

Secure the edges of the sheep's body to the background patch with white thread, making a series of lines to suggest the texture of the coat. With green thread, embroider grass on the top edge of the hill in the same manner.

Freely stitch flowers and grass on the ground, varying the zigzag width according to their shapes. Stems are made by zigzagging a series of straight lines from left to right along the stem lines.

Iron the patch onto the jeans. Raise the feed dogs on the machine, tighten tension, and set the machine for a medium-wide zigzag stitch. Satin-stitch the patch to the jeans around the edges.

Buttonhole Dress

Shown on page 30.

MATERIALS
Commercial dress pattern
Dress fabric and notions
 required by pattern
Brightly colored buttons and
 threads

INSTRUCTIONS
 Cut out the dress according to the commercial pattern instructions. Stitch brightly colored buttonholes of varying lengths in a random manner on the front dress section only. Assemble the dress following the instructions with the commercial pattern.
 Sew buttons to a few selected buttonholes for added color.

Personalized Infant's Layette

Shown on page 32.

MATERIALS
Commercial pattern for layette
Fabric yardages required by
 pattern
Sewing threads
Assorted ribbons

INSTRUCTIONS
 Cut out fabric pieces for the layette using commercial pattern. With pencil or water-soluble transfer pen, write the baby's name on selected pieces such as yoke or bib front.
 Set your sewing machine for a medium-wide zigzag stitch. Slip typing paper under the fabric to be embroidered with the name and satin-stitch over the letters. Remove paper.
 Assemble the garments according to the commercial pattern instructions.
 Add finishing touches with ribbons and ties.

Crazy-Patch Child's Vest

Shown on page 33.

MATERIALS
Commercial vest pattern
Vest fabric according to pattern
 requirements
Fabric scraps, lace, and ribbon
 scraps
Assorted sewing threads

INSTRUCTIONS
 Cut out vest pieces using commerical pattern. From fabric scraps, cut crazy-patch shapes. Turn under raw edges and baste them next to each other on the main vest pieces. Add strips of ribbon for contrast.
 With decorative machine stitches, sew along the edges of all pieces, varying thread colors and stitching patterns. Add lace scraps where desired and zigzag in place.
 Assemble the vest according to pattern instructions.

Victorian Dolls

Shown on page 33.

MATERIALS
½ yard fabric (large doll's dress)
⅛ yard fabric (sleeve and hem
 ruffles for large doll)
¼ yard fabric (small doll's dress)
⅛ yard fabric (sleeve and hem
 ruffles for small doll)
¼ yard skin-tone fabric
⅛ yard tan fabric (hair backing)
⅔ yard solid-color backing fabric
Scrap of black satin (shoes)
Matching sewing threads
1 yard 1½-inch-wide flat lace
2 yards ½-inch-wide flat lace
¾ yard ⅝-inch-wide flat lace
7 skeins tan heavy cotton pearl
 floss (hair)
Assorted embroidery flosses,
 ribbons
Small pearls
1 pound polyester fiberfill
1 yard fusible webbing
Tracing paper, typing paper
Water-soluble transfer pen

INSTRUCTIONS

To prepare materials
 Enlarge the pattern, page 40, onto tracing paper; for doll backs flop the patterns, trace again, leaving out faces and substituting hair. Tape designs to a well-lighted window. Tape the backing fabric on top of the design and trace the outlines of the dolls and arms with the transfer pen, spacing them 2 inches apart. Mark the placement of all appliqué shapes.
 Cut out, adding ¾-inch seam allowances around the pieces. Cut matching arm backs from backing fabric. Cut apart tracing paper pattern for appliqué pattern pieces and pin them to fabrics.
 From skin-tone fabric, cut the arms ¼ inch longer than the pattern where arm meets sleeve (this allows the sleeve to overlap slightly when appliquéing). Cut the lower legs so the skin-toned fabric will extend behind the shoes. All other pieces are cut on pattern lines; they will be butted against each other jigsaw-puzzle fashion.
 Transfer all stitching lines to appliqué pieces and mark facial details.

To make large doll
 Secure face and hair backing to the backing fabric with basting or fusible webbing. Set machine for a narrow zigzag and stitch raw edges of hair backing with matching thread. Satin-stitch the lower edge of the doll's face with skin-colored thread.
 Baste or fuse the legs in place. Attach satin shoes over the top and zigzag around the raw edges with black thread. Satin-stitch around the raw edges of the ankles with matching thread.
 Sew ⅝-inch lace over the tops of the ankles for pantaloons, layering and stitching from the bottom to the top; extend the top layer into the dress ruffle area.
 continued

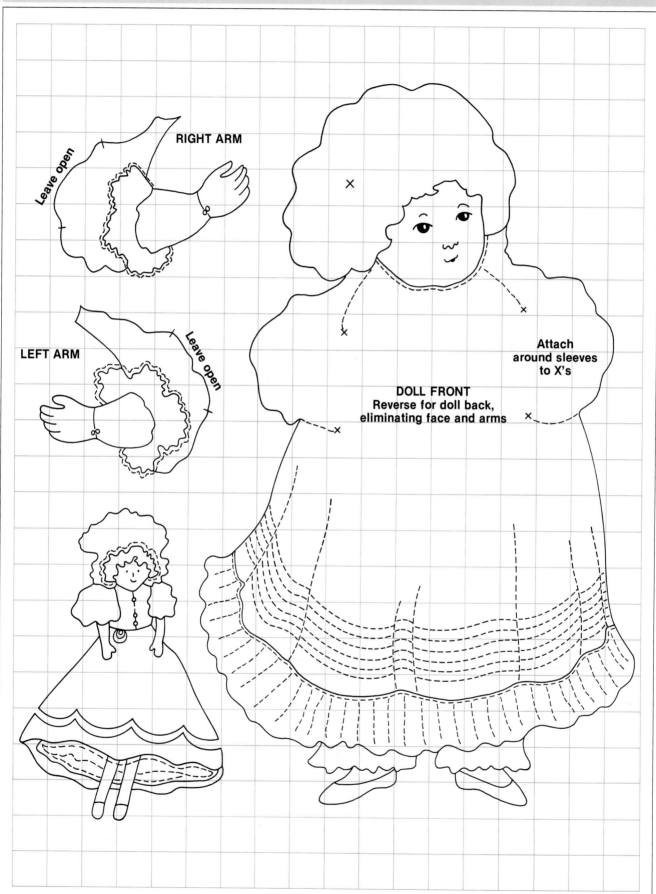

RIGHT ARM

Leave open

LEFT ARM

Leave open

Attach around sleeves to X's

DOLL FRONT
Reverse for doll back,
eliminating face and arms

1 Square = 1 Inch

Trim the lace on the outside edges as necessary to correspond with marked lines on the backing fabric. Zigzag around the outside and lower edges of the lace area.

Baste or fuse the lower dress ruffle in place. With a narrow zigzag stitch and matching thread, satin-stitch over the vertical lines and around the side and lower edges of the ruffle. Place a row of ½-inch lace edging to the top of the ruffle and zigzag over the top edge with matching thread.

Pin the main dress piece in place. Lay 6 strands of embroidery floss over the horizontal lines at the bottom of the dress and couch over them with a narrow zigzag stitch. Change to thread matching the dress and satin-stitch the vertical lines at the dress bottom. Zigzag around the outside edges of the dress.

For the doll back, attach hair backing to doll backing fabric with zigzagging. Continue the appliqué procedure as for the front.

For the arm fronts, baste or fuse the skin-tone fabric onto the backing fabric. Satin-stitch with matching thread around all edges except where the arms meet sleeves; stitch the fingers.

Lay the sleeve ruffle on the area indicated on the pattern; insert a strip of ½-inch lace behind the outside edge and baste or fuse in place. Satin-stitch with matching thread around the raw edges of the ruffles.

Pin arm fronts to arm backs, right sides facing. With a straight stitch, sew ⅛ inch outside of satin-stitching, leaving open the areas indicated on the pattern. Clip curves, trim seams, and turn. A narrow edge of backing fabric will be visible around the arms. Stuff lightly with fiberfill and sew closed.

Embroider the doll's face using 2 strands of floss.

Baste the arms to the dress (see diagram); satin-stitch around the outside edges to Xs. Tack hands together at the fingertips.

Pin the doll front to the back, right sides facing. With a straight stitch, sew around all edges ⅛ inch from satin-stitching, leaving an opening for turning. Clip curves, trim seams; turn. Stuff to desired plumpness and sew opening closed.

For hair, cut 6 to 8 strands of pearl cotton floss each 36 inches long. Beginning at the neck edge, tack the loose ends in place with one strand of floss. With the strands held together, make a loop over your index finger and stitch them down with floss. Do not cut the strands. Continue to make loops, tacking them in place until area is covered.

To shape the chin, hand-sew small stitches from the front, through the neck, to the back.

Gather wide lace and tack 2 layers by hand to back and front neck edges, placing the underneath layer ¼ inch lower than the top. Hand-stitch a row of ½-inch lace at the top edge of the wide neckline lace.

To make small doll

Baste or fuse all fabric pieces in place on the front and back of the backing fabric. With narrow zigzagging, satin-stitch around all pieces with matching thread around all pieces. Satin-stitch hat lines on front and back.

Add small strips of lace to the bodice front and stitch in place. Beginning with the lower layer of the petticoat, baste and satin-stitch the top edge of a ½-inch strip of lace; add layers, stitching as before. Zigzag lace to hat front and back. Embroider face.

To make the shoes, satin-stitch along shoe lines with thread matching the lower dress. Fill in the toe area with a free zigzag stitch.

To assemble the doll, pin the front to the back, right sides facing. Machine-stitch around the edge ⅛ inch outside of satin stitching, leaving an opening for turning. Trim seams, turn.

Stuff doll lightly with fiberfill and sew the opening closed. To attach hair, use 1 strand of heavy cotton pearl floss. Make small, consecutive loops, attaching each with matching sewing thread.

Add a ribbon bow and lace rosette to the hat back. Make small slits through the doll's waist at sides and insert a narrow ribbon with a needle from front to back. Tie in the back and add another ribbon; tie in a bow.

Tack small bows and pearls to the scallops on the lower dress; add a small rosette to the waist front. Attach pearls to the bodice and a bow to the front of the hat.

Painter's Smock

Shown on page 34.

MATERIALS
Purchased or handmade smock
⅓ yard of striped fabric (palette)
Assorted solid-color fabrics (paints, brushes)
Assorted sewing threads
2½ yards navy double-fold bias tape
Tracing paper, typing paper

INSTRUCTIONS
Enlarge the pattern, *below*, onto tracing paper. Place another sheet of tracing paper over the design and trace the brushes. Then, moving the paper as it is needed, *continued*

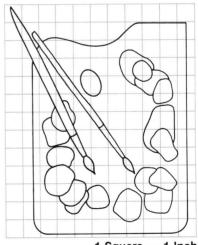

1 Square = 1 Inch

trace each individual paint area onto the tracing paper, completing the shapes; these will be overlapped when they are appliquéd to the palette.

Cut the brushes and paint shapes from fusible webbing and from fabrics of assorted colors.

Cut the palette from striped fabric. Cover the outside edge and the hole edge with bias tape.

Referring to the design, fuse the paint shapes to the palette, overlapping them where indicated. With a tightly spaced, medium-wide zigzag stitch and matching thread, satin-stitch around the raw edges of the paint shapes.

Sew the palette and hole to the smock with a straight stitch along the outside edge of the bias tape. Attach the brushes to the top of the palette with fusible webbing. Then, satin-stitch with matching thread around all raw edges.

Color-Name Appliqués

Shown on page 34.

MATERIALS
Commericial patterns for child's jumper and jumpsuit
Pale, solid-color fabrics in yellow, red, blue, green, purple, and pink according to pattern requirements (basic garments)
Bright red, green, blue, yellow, pink, and purple appliqué fabric scraps
Matching threads
Purchased letter stencils
1 yard fusible webbing
Water-soluble transfer pen

INSTRUCTIONS
Cut out garment pieces using commercial patterns, referring to the photograph on page 34 for color placement. Place letter stencils for the color names on top of corresponding appliqué scraps; trace the letters with a transfer pen. Cut letters from fabric and fusible webbing.

Fuse color names to the jumper and jumpsuit pieces. Set machine for medium-wide satin stitches and zigzag around all raw edges of the letters with matching thread.

Assemble garments according to pattern instructions.

Embroidered Sheet and Pillowcase

Shown on page 35.

MATERIALS
Purchased sheet, pillowcase
Letter stencils
Assorted sewing threads
Spray starch, typing paper
Water-soluble transfer pen

INSTRUCTIONS
Spray-starch the areas to be embroidered. With the transfer pen, trace the letters onto the sheet and pillowcase.

To embroider
Set your sewing machine for a wide, closely spaced zigzag stitch; two or more rows of stitching may be necessary, depending upon the width of the letters.

Place typing paper underneath the area to be embroidered. Satin-stitch selected letters or parts of letters with one color of thread; change to another color and continue in the same manner, overlapping stitches at diagonal corners of letters.

To finish
When embroidery is completed, remove typing paper and tie all threads on the back of the fabric.

Place the sheet and pillowcase right side down on a soft surface; spray-starch and press.

Basketball Dolls

Shown on page 36.

MATERIALS
⅔ yard each of black felt, muslin
⅛ yard of white felt
Fabric scraps in assorted solids and prints
Assorted sewing threads
Purchased star appliqué (optional)
½ pound polyester fiberfill
1 yard fusible webbing
Water-soluble transfer pen

INSTRUCTIONS
Enlarge the patterns, page 43, onto paper.

To prepare materials
From muslin, cut out the doll bodies along the outermost pattern lines and transfer the faces to muslin with a water-soluble transfer pen.

Cut patterns apart. Pin hair and clothing pieces to selected fabrics and fusible webbing. Cut out on pattern lines without seam allowances. Pieces will fit together in a jigsaw-puzzle fashion.
Note: For a perfect match, cut out felt and fusible webbing layers all at once.

For the basketball, cut out the basic shape from tan fabric; cut out black strips from felt strips.

1 Square = 3 Inches

To appliqué the dolls

Set machine for a tightly spaced, medium zigzag stitch. Place the doll faces on top of typing paper and satin-stitch over the facial features with black thread. Remove paper.

Fuse the hair and clothing pieces to the muslin doll bodies. Satin-stitch over all interior raw edges only; outside edges of the dolls will be satin-stitched later to the felt backing.

Change your sewing machine to straight stitching and sew the star and letter appliqués to the doll shirts. Stitch outlines of the star and letters, expanding the design outward at ¼-inch intervals. If desired, add free machine stitching to shirt sleeves and other areas, to enhance the design.

Pin or baste the muslin doll bodies to the black felt fabric. Satin-stitch around the outside edges of the dolls, stuffing as you stitch. Cut out ¼ inch from outermost stitching lines.

Fuse black felt strips over the ball front. Satin-stitch interior raw edges. Place the appliquéd ball on black felt and finish as for the dolls.

Brag Jacket

Shown on page 37.

MATERIALS
Purchased jacket
Sports badges, patches
Sports letters, pins
Purchased appliqués
Sewing threads

INSTRUCTIONS

Pin or baste the badges, patches, and award letters to the jacket. With your machine set on either a straight or zigzag stitch, appliqué around all raw edges.

CUTWORK REPERTOIRE

♦ ♦ ♦

Now you can achieve the look of handmade cutwork embroidery precisely and speedily with zigzag stitching. Although most cutwork is challenging and time consuming, the sewing machine technique can save you valuable time in the process and reward you with the handsome look of contemporary stitchery.

To duplicate the ring-of-flowers tablecloth on this page, use your appliqué skills for decorating the corners with their bright blooms before working the cutwork leaf borders. Handy actual-size patterns are provided on page 52 to get you off to a quick start; you can trace them directly from the pages of the book.

For a simpler cutwork idea, see the pristine cutout place mat on page 48. Made of two layers of white organdy and a layer of white interfacing, it is shadow-quilted before its edges are finished with a minimum of cutwork.

The openwork linen borders on pages 50–51 are a worthy challenge for an intermediate stitcher. Step-by-step photographs show you exactly what happens in the process.

So shine up your machine and pick a project! In no time at all you can learn several more ways to use your machine creatively.

LACY CUTWORK TABLECLOTH

When you set your table with the beautiful cloth shown on this page, *far right*, you'll be sure to hear a compliment or two!

After appliquéing the colorful flowers on the corners, it's a good idea to practice making cutwork leaves on scrap fabric. Once you've mastered the skill of making one leaf, you're ready to work the entire tablecloth.

To make a cutwork leaf, slip typing paper under the traced motif for stability. Then, place lengths of white embroidery floss across the vein lines on the leaf and satin-stitch across the strands of floss, *near right, top*. Trim floss ends away and satin-stitch around the leaf outline.

Cut away the insides of the leaves between vein sections, *near right, bottom,* being

careful not to cut satin stitches. Satin-stitch over all previous stitching to stabilize the lines on the leaf. Pull sewing threads to wrong side of fabric and tie off. Remove paper.

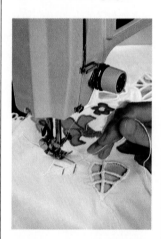

CHILD'S DRESS-UP PINAFORE

Children love the excitement of getting dressed up. The crisp holly cutwork apron shown here is sophisticated stitchery that is perfect for a special occasion.

Cutwork leaves, satin-stitch line work, trapunto holly berries, and an irregular hem on a clean, white fabric make up the subtle white-on-white design.

To make this charming pinafore for a very special little person you can put what you learned on page 46 to good use.

Then see the photograph, *below,* to finish the hem.

For the unusual cutout hem, loosely zigzag along the hem outline to stabilize it. Then cut away the fabric just outside the stitch line. With your machine set on a medium-wide, close satin-stitch, cover the previous stitch line. Repeat the stitching once again for a precise, rounded finish.

SHADOW-APPLIQUÉD PLACE MAT

Nothing matches the formal elegance of white table linens. The pure color and design of the place mat *above* contrasts dramatically with the dark wood grain beneath it and provides a perfect backdrop for dressy crystal and silver.

Stitched together with a combination of cutwork techniques and shadow-appliqué, the tranquil symmetry of the place mat's design is formed by sandwiching a layer of white shapes—cut from interfacing—between two layers of pure-white organdy.

To make the place mat, pin and baste the three layers of fabric together and slip the place mat under the needle on the machine. Stitching just outside of the interfacing shapes, quilt the layers of the place mat together.

Finish the place mat with zigzag satin stitching as for the cutwork apron shown on page 47. Complete instructions for the place mats are on pages 54–55.

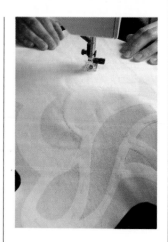

POSY PLACE MAT

Whether used as a place mat or as a centerpiece, the colorful nosegay, *right*, is just the ticket for a festive table.

To duplicate it, combine your appliqué and cutwork skills with lots of colored threads and fabrics. The results will no doubt be well worth the stitching time you spend.

And just in case you'd rather start with something small, try the nosegay's companion coaster (see the upper righthand corner of the photograph). Use only the center flower from the place mat design, but enlarge the scale.

The coaster is shown in progress in the photograph *at right.* When the appliqué work is nearly complete, cut through all fabric layers to make the cutouts at the flower center.

Finish the edges of the cutouts as well as the coaster edge with closely spaced, medium-wide satin stitches. Complete instructions for the coaster and place mat are found on page 55.

BORDERING LINENS WITH OPENWORK

The simplest of sewing materials—fabric and thread—are the makings for the elegant linen borders shown *at right*.

The lovely needle woven bands define the edges of the sheet and pillowcase in a straightforward fashion, and turn ordinary white-sale goods into luxury linens. Besides looking attractive they demonstrate beautifully that simplicity is best.

To make the open cutwork borders, begin with white woven-fabric strips. Draw out two horizontal threads to mark the band and remove all of the horizontal threads inside the marked band, *upper right*.

Then, zigzag over the vertical threads that remain in the band, collecting three or four threads in each stitching to form sturdy vertical cords across the entire openwork band.

Using the diagram on page 57 as a stitching guide, cross over the vertical cords with lines of straight stitching and zigzagging, making the latticework design, *center right*.

To finish, insert the band in a purchased sheet and pillowcase, *bottom right*.

Complete instructions for the openwork bands follow on pages 56–57.

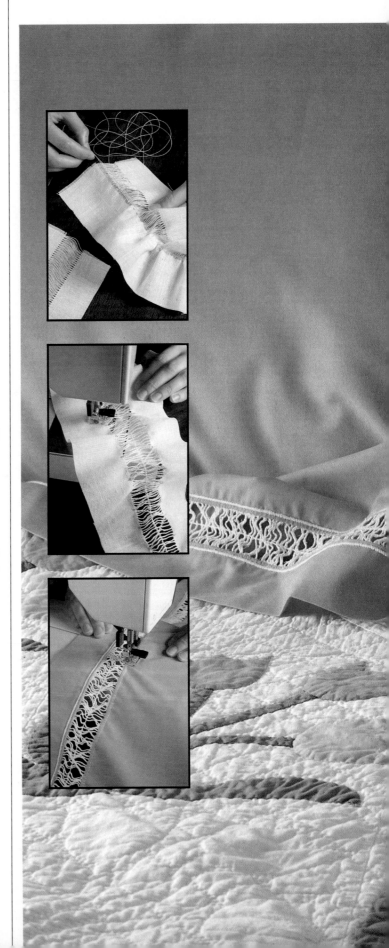

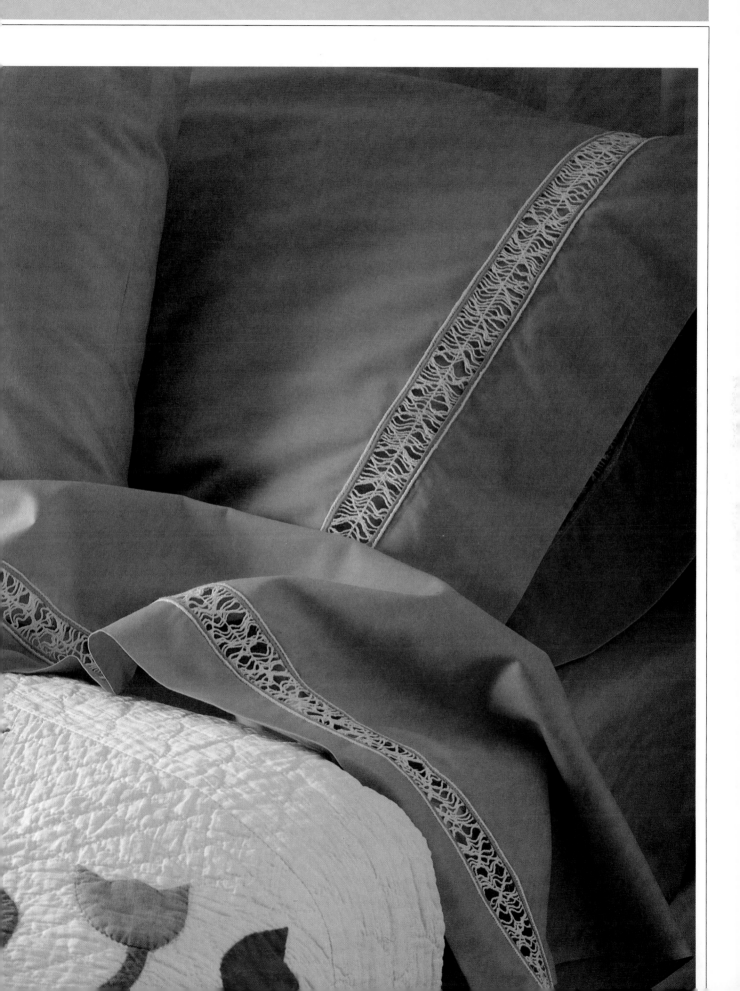

CUTWORK REPERTOIRE

Full-size

Ring-of-flowers Tablecloth

Shown on page 44.

Finished size is 54 inches square.

MATERIALS
54-inch square of high-quality white fabric such as cotton or a closely woven blend
10 spools white thread
½ yard fusible webbing
Scraps of pastel fabrics
Matching pastel threads
3 skeins of white embroidery floss
6 yards of decorative lace
Water-soluble transfer pen
Typing paper, butcher paper

INSTRUCTIONS
Trace full-size appliqué patterns, page 52, onto paper; cut out. Follow the diagram, *below*, for placement of the design elements. To transfer the appliqués and cutwork to the tablecloth, draw around actual-size patterns with transfer pen, leaving 3½-inch margins between the border design and tablecloth edge.

Cut appliqué flowers from pastel scraps; cut duplicate shapes from fusible webbing. (See cutting and fusing photographs on page 46 for additonal help). Fuse flowers onto tablecloth fabric with iron, then machine-appliqué all raw edges in matching threads.

To make each cutwork leaf, slip typing paper under traced motif for stability. Place 6-strand embroidery floss along leaf "veins." Using a wide, dense stitching setting, satin-stitch over floss to cover the embroidery floss.

Carefully trim floss ends away; satin-stitch around leaf outline, omitting floss. Repeat this procedure for all leaves, inserting fresh typing paper whenever needed. When all are stitched, remove paper scraps from the underside.

Cut away the insides of the leaves between the vein sections, being careful not to cut the satin stitching.

Satin-stitch over all previous satin stitching to hide frayed edges and to stabilize the lines on the leaves.

To hem tablecloth, trim raw edges of the cloth and turn under ¼ inch. With zigzag stitches set a narrow stitch width and a long stitch length, sew along raw edges. Fold hem over again ½ inch and press. Blindstitch hem by hand with tiny stitches.

Attach purchased lace trim to edges of tablecloth with small stitches, sewing it to tablecloth only at the uppermost edges of the lace.

Steam-press on the wrong side of the tablecloth to finish.

Child's Dress-Up Pinafore

Shown on page 47.

MATERIALS
1 yard of white oxford cloth or medium-weight cotton
Scraps of fiberfill or quilt batting
Sharp embroidery scissors
White sewing thread
Water-soluble marking pen

INSTRUCTIONS
From white fabric, cut an 8-inch square for the pinafore bib, a 15x18-inch rectangle for the skirt, two 2x13½-inch strips for the waistband, four 1¾x15½-inch pieces for the pinafore straps, and four 3½x26-inch pieces for ties.

Apron skirt
Enlarge the design, page 54, *top*, onto paper and transfer it to the skirt square. With a medium-close stitch setting, zigzag-stitch over the lines.

For the trapunto holly berries, back the berry areas with scraps of fabric and batting. Stitch over
continued

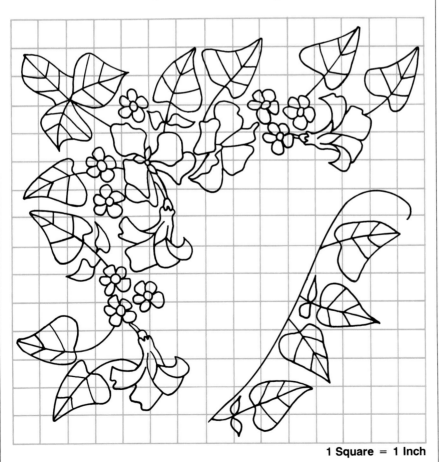

1 Square = 1 Inch

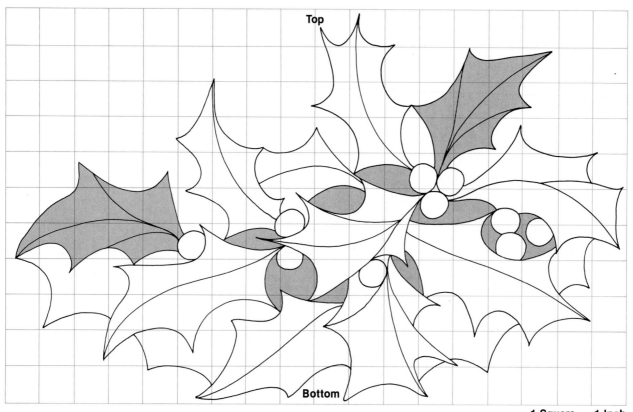

Top

Bottom

1 Square = 1 Inch

the entire design again, catching backing fabric in the stitches around the berries. Trim excess fabric and batting on the back.

With a sharp scissors, cut away the holly leaves designated by the shaded areas on the diagram; trim the irregular hem close to the stitching. To finish, widen the zigzag stitch slightly and sew over previous zigzag stitching along all cut-away edges. Be sure all frayed threads are caught up into this final stitching.

Apron bib

Enlarge the design, *below*, and transfer it to bib square. Work the design as for the skirt.

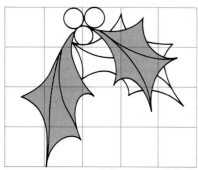

1 Square = 1 Inch

Assembling the pinafore

Finish the skirt sides with rolled hems on the machine or by hand; finish the bib top and sides with the same. With right sides facing, use ¼-inch seams to stitch one waistband strip to the skirt.

Stitch the ties together with right sides facing and leave an opening in the end of each tie for turning. Turn, press, and pleat the open end to fit the waistband. Stitch the ties to the band.

With right sides facing, sew the straps; leave openings for turning. Turn right side out and press. Stitch openings closed and sew straps to bib top.

Fold under the ends of each strap 2 inches (adjust to fit child) to make loops for the ties; stitch. Sew bib and inner waistband to top edge of waistband; turn band down and hand-sew to apron. Thread ties through loops.

Shadow-Quilted Place Mat

Shown on page 48.

Finished size is 14½x19 inches.

MATERIALS
1⅞ yard white 45-inch-wide cotton organdy
2 yards white medium-heavy nonfusible interfacing
White sewing thread, size 60
Size 11 sewing machine needle
Butcher paper
Carbon paper
Lightweight cardboard or heavy paper such as tagboard
Water-soluble transfer pen
Razor blade
Fine sewing needle

INSTRUCTIONS

Note: The materials list indicates amounts needed to make two place mats.

Preparing the pattern

Enlarge pattern, *below,* onto paper. Trace the design onto heavy paper with carbon paper. Working with the heavy paper, use a razor blade to carefully cut away the pattern's shaded areas. Cut out the pattern around the perimeter.

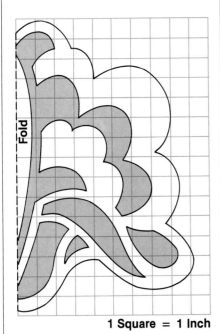

1 Square = 1 Inch

Preparing the shadow-panel

Lay the cut-out pattern of the place mat on the interfacing. Draw around the paper shapes onto interfacing with a transfer pen. With sharp scissors, carefully cut away *shaded* shapes, discarding them. You will have one narrow center section and one large outer shape for each mat.

Wash and iron organdy.

On the straight grain of the fabric, arrange the shadow-panel pieces on one layer of organdy. Be sure to leave 1-inch margins between the place mats. Lay a second layer of organdy over the shadow panels.

Pin and cut out place mats, leaving ½-inch margins around the place mat's perimeters.

1 Square = 1 Inch

Assembling the place mats

Baste through all thicknesses with a fine needle and long running stitches.

Machine-quilt the place mats just outside of all interfacing (shadow-panel) shapes. Use a stitch length of 1½.

Stitch on exterior edge of each place mat, catching the edges of the interfacing shapes. Bring all threads to wrong side, tie and cut; or, tie and weave ends through stitches on back side.

Finishing

Trim close to the stitching on the outer edges of the place mats.

Set machine for narrow zigzag satin stitches. Overcast the outer edges (perimeters) of the place mats, making a fine, precise edge with satin stitching.

Remove basting threads, handwash to remove marks from transfer pen, and iron the mats.

Posy Place Mats

Shown on page 49.

Finished size for place mat is approximately 16x17 inches. Coaster size is 5½x6 inches.

MATERIALS

Note: The list below provides materials for two place mats and two coasters.
1 yard of 18-inch-wide fusible webbing
1 yard of 18-inch-wide lightweight iron-on interfacing
½ yard of 45-inch-wide light green linen-look fabric
½ yard of 45-inch-wide light pink linen-look fabric
¼ yard each of dark green, white, fuschia, light aqua, and dark aqua linen-look fabrics
Pink, dark green, fuschia, light aqua, dark aqua, and white sewing threads
Butcher paper, tissue paper
Water-soluble transfer pen
Paper towels, typing paper

continued

INSTRUCTIONS

Preparing the pattern

Enlarge the posy pattern, page 55, onto butcher paper to make a master pattern. For coaster, use a scale of 1 square = ⅔ inch and enlarge *only* the center posy and 5 dark green leaves.

Trace the enlarged patterns onto tissue paper to make cutting patterns. Cut out all pieces, marking them for color, and throw away all light green pieces. See the photograph on page 49 for a color guide.

Preparing the materials

Cut the light green yardage in half to make two 18-inch squares. Tape the light green pieces (place mats) to a well-lighted window. Slip the master pattern for the place mat underneath the fabric and trace the design onto the fabric with transfer pen.

For coasters, transfer the design onto two pieces of white fabric as for the place mats.

Fuse the iron-on interfacing to the wrong sides of the place mats and coasters.

Cutting the posies

Note: The pieces of the appliqué fit together in a jigsaw-puzzle fashion. There is no need to add turning allowances to the shapes.

Using cut apart tissue paper pattern pieces, pin central posies on a layer of pink fabric and fusible webbing. Cut out. Repeat for second place mat and coasters.

Position the pink posies in their places on the green and white background fabrics with the fusible webbing pieces sandwiched between the fabrics.

Fuse the layers together with a warm iron, following the fusing instructions supplied with the webbing. (*Note:* Place a paper towel between the fabric and iron to catch stray wisps of webbing.)

Continue cutting and fusing the dark green leaves and all small flowers, leaving the light green shapes of the place mats untouched.

When all pieces are fused in place, draw in the detail lines for outlining and cutwork with the transfer pen.

Stitching the appliqués

Loosely zigzag over all raw edges, attaching fabrics to the interfacing layer.

Set your machine for medium-wide satin stitching, and sew over all detail lines and loosely stitched raw edges. Note the thread colors in the photograph on page 49. Zigzag outside edges of the place mats and coasters again for a finished look.

Note: Slip typing paper under light green leaf edges when stitching. The paper will stabilize the fabric and the stitchery.

Cutwork

With a sharp scissors, cut out circles and flower centers, being careful not to cut stitches. Satin-stitch over previous stitching to finish the cutwork.

Openwork Sheet and Pillowcase Borders

Shown on pages 50–51.

MATERIALS

⅓ yard of white 60-inch-wide, loosely woven, linenlike fabric with strong warp and weft threads
White thread
Cotton string
Water-soluble transfer pen
Tweezers

INSTRUCTIONS

Pulling threads

Cut fabric horizontally into 4½-inch strips. Cut off the selvage ends. Make one strip two times the width of the pillowcase, plus add 1 inch for seam allowances. For the sheet, cut enough strips to make up the width plus 2 inches; pieces will be joined together.

Pull off some of the threads along the raw edges so approximately ¼ inch of loose crosswise threads appear.

Near an end of one strip, measure 1¾ inch from long edge of strip and mark a dot with the transfer pen.

Grasp a thread at this dot with tweezers and begin pulling carefully until it is long enough to be held by fingers. Then, holding thread with fingers, continue pulling gently, winding it around your index finger and smoothing gathers a little at a time with other hand until thread is completely pulled out.

If thread breaks, pull out broken thread and use a needle to pick up remainder of the thread about ¼ inch from breaking point. Measure 1¼ inch from this line and mark a dot on the edge. Pull out another thread. This defines the openwork area for the needlewoven band.

Repeat for all bands.

Machine-stitch (stay-stitch) on these lines to secure band area. Knot the thread ends by hand or by machine.

Pull threads out of fabric between the machine-stitched lines. After several have been removed, 2 or 3 threads can be pulled out at one time, if desired. Continue pulling out threads until all warp threads are exposed between machine-stitched lines.

After completion, join drawn thread strips together by placing the fabric right sides together, lining up the open threads, and machine-stitching a ¼-inch seam.

From the wrong side, clip off any extra warp threads in the seam margin area only.

Join enough strips to complete the width necessary to trim pillowcase and sheet.

Needle-weaving the bands

Set machine for narrow zigzag (feed dogs may be lowered, if desired). Loosen pressure foot tension, if necessary.

Beginning at the top left edge of the open band and holding top and bottom of strip firmly, zigzag downward quickly, catching several threads at one time. With needle in fabric, turn strip and move stitching over to the next several threads. Zigzag to beginning position. Repeat procedure until band is completed.

If any single threads remain within the band, they may be clipped off so only the thick vertical cords remain.

With marking pen, place dots 1 inch apart on upper and lower edge of band, directly across from each other. See diagram, *below*, for marking.

Set machine for straight stitching. Sew a horizontal line across all vertical cords at the center of the open band (see diagram). Stitch over the line several times.

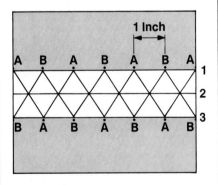

Then, beginning at the first dot on the top of the band, sew diagonally across the cords, connecting all A dots and skipping all B dots.

This will result in a zigzag pattern from one edge to the other. Stitch over this line several times.

Repeat the procedure, connecting all B dots and creating an X pattern (see diagram). Be sure to intersect the lines at the center points. Machine-stitch several times over this line.

Change machine stitch to narrow zigzag, and zigzag over all of these lines so they appear similar in thickness to original vertical cording.

Zigzag with a medium-wide stitch over edges of band.

Note: Zigzagging will change the vertical cording to wavy lines. Band will appear somewhat puckered until fabric is trimmed off the band.

Trim off excess fabric next to zigzagging. Press the band.

Repeat for pillowcase band.

Inserting the bands

SHEET: Decide on the placement for the band. Mark a cutting line on the top edge of sheet, allowing an extra ½ inch for the seam margin; cut.

On the right side of the cut-off sheet strip, lay one band edge ½ inch from cut edge. Stitch in place, then zigzag with a close stitch. Flip band so the ½-inch margin folds over on the wrong side of the sheet. On the right side of the sheet, topstitch approximately ¼ inch from the fold.

Turn to the wrong side. Fold up ¼ inch of the seam margin once, then once again so the raw zigzagged edge of band is covered and sandwiched between the folded front edge of the sheet and the folded back margin. Baste.

On the right side of the sheet, lay cording over the stitching and zigzag over the cording.

Place the band (with the upper sheet strip attached), right side down on the right side of the lower part of the sheet, ½ inch from the top. Stitch, then zigzag in place. Continue the procedure as for the other edge.

PILLOWCASE: Open the seams on the pillowcase sides. Repeat the band insertion procedure as for the sheet, *above*. Close the side seams to finish.

Sewing Machine Upkeep

Whether your sewing machine is a top-of-the-line model or an old reliable, it's worth keeping in A-1 working order. Here are a few tips for trouble-free sewing.

Knowing your machine

Read up on the dos and don'ts of your model in the manual that came with it. Get to know what's what and how to troubleshoot when a problem arises. You may even be surprised to learn all that your machine can do.

Removing dust and lint

Every time you sew, bits of lint and fiber accumulate around the bobbin case, feed dogs, and moving parts. Before beginning a sewing project, remove the machine's throat plate and brush away the built-up lint.

Oiling the machine

A periodic oiling keeps the machine running freely and reduces friction and wear. If your machine gets heavy use every day, oil it daily. But if you're a weekend seamster, an oiling every other week will suffice. (*Note:* Remove all dust and lint *before* oiling the machine.) Never drench your machine with oil. Use a drop or two at each point indicated in your sewing machine's manual. Then run the machine slowly for several minutes so the oil can gradually work its way into the moving parts. Remove excess oil from the thread-handling parts with any lint-free cloth or cheesecloth.

FANCIFUL TRIMS

♦ ♦ ♦

An innovative stitcher sees trim potential in anything that can be stitched down. Buttons, bows, beads, fabric patches badges, embroidered tapes, laces, and ribbons are all natural candidates for imaginative embellishment. And the list needn't end there; you can find great ways to use patterned fabrics, novelty yarns, and cords, as well as interesting bits and pieces cut from throw-aways. On the next few pages you'll see ways to put your trim collections to good use.

A stitcher with romantic inclinations created the regal Elizabethan jacket on these pages. The billowy leg-of-mutton sleeves exhibit an unusual approach to trimming: The sleeves are not merely *decorated* with ribbons; they are *made* of ribbons. Single lengths of beautiful ribbons, butted and joined together with zigzag stitches, combine to form the fabric used to make the sleeves.

When teamed with the plush velvet jacket bodice and wide velvet cuffs, the fanciful ribbon sleeves become a splendid embellishment for the finished garment. Complete instructions for the jacket are on page 66.

FANCIFUL TRIMS

COUCHED SKIRT AND CUTWORK BLOUSE

The stunning and sassy skirt *opposite* is no slouch when it comes to trimming. And it proves that even the most common approach to decorating clothing—stitching trim to fabric—can look extraordinary.

Couched metallic cords, stitched down in a free and simple style, are the makings for the skirt's trimwork.

Just cut lengths of the cording and position them in desired lines on the fabric. With sewing thread and a minimum of zigzag stitches, sew over the cording to hold it in place.

Consider a trim that becomes an integral part of the fabric it decorates. Sewing machine thread works with the threads of woven fabric to make the delicate cutwork trim on the elegant blouse, *above*.

To learn how to do simple cutwork, turn to page 46. Practice the technique on scrap fabric with regular sewing thread. Then, after mastering the basics, you can work this refined design in a rayon thread.

For more cutwork design inspirations, visit museums showing exhibits of hand-stitched cutwork. You can find endless possibilities to translate into machine trimwork by simplifying the motifs that you see.

FANCIFUL TRIMS

SCRAP COLLECTOR'S PILLOW PORTRAITS

Here's your chance to pull out all the stops—and your collection of buttons, ribbons, and old jewelry! For a truly fun trimming extravaganza, stitch one or all of these pillow portraits from the infamous court of King Henry VIII.

Borrowed from the original 16th century paintings by Hans Holbein, the figures make a dramatic appearance in appliquéd fabrics and richly embellished finery, and prove that anything in trimming is possible. Dimensions for the pillows are about 24x28 inches.

To begin these pillows for your own castle, collect fabric scraps of brocades, velveteen, satins, and chiffons as well as bits of lacy trims and golden cords.

For a closer look at the trimmings on Henry and his fourth wife, Anne of Cleves, please turn the page.

PILLOW PORTRAITS

There's no limit to the possibilities for trimming up a portrait such as Henry's, *left.* The original painting of Henry, richly embellished with the elaborate fabrics of the court, suggests ideas for trimming; the decorative clothing of the portrait translates easily into contemporary materials.

For example, a fabric printed with many fine details suggests a heavily embroidered shirt front, an actual feather makes Henry's hat plume. And an old button is a simple replacement for the original heavily engraved gold medallion necklace. All of these ideas are shortcuts to great results with very little work.

Anne of Cleves, sent her portrait to the court of Henry before their marriage. She appears again in the pillow *above,* recreated with fabrics and trims.

To make your own pillow portraits, use the examples pictured here, but feel free to make your own personal interpretations of the designs drawn on pages 68–69. Take advantage of the materials and trims you find available, whether they're discovered in jewelry boxes, flea markets, or cut from throwaway clothing.

Renaissance Ribbon Jacket

Shown on page 58.

MATERIALS
Commerical jacket pattern
Teal velveteen fabric, lining, and notions as specified in pattern
Ribbons in the following amounts and colors:
¼-inch-wide single-face satin ribbon— 4 yards grape; 4½ yards plum; 4½ yards wine; 3¾ yards teal; 3¼ yards jade
⅞-inch-wide velvet ribbons— 2 yards red; 3¼ yards violet; 1¼ yards burgundy
⅛-inch-wide metallic grosgrain ribbon— 27 yards gold
Five ¾-inch gold buttons

INSTRUCTIONS
Follow instructions given in the commercial pattern for making the jacket body and cuffs.

To make the ribbon fabric for the sleeves, begin with a base fabric to attach the ribbons onto. Cut two sleeves from teal velveteen.

Cut several ribbon lengths and pin them to the velveteen sleeves, beginning at the sleeve centers and working outward. Leave ⅛-inch spaces between each ribbon for gold ribbon inserts.

Using a zigzag stitch on your machine and strong teal thread, stitch the ribbons in place, making sure to keep them straight and perpendicular to the sleeve edges. As you sew, the ribbons will pucker, adding to the texture of the fabric.

When the ribbons are stitched in place, zigzag-stitch the gold metallic ribbon between each colored ribbon.

Finish the jacket according to pattern directions.

Couched Skirt

Shown on page 60.

MATERIALS
Commercial skirt pattern
Ecru gabardine or chino fabric to match yardage listed on pattern
Notions for skirt
Ecru sewing thread
50 yards of washable gold metallic cording
Gold sewing thread

INSTRUCTIONS
Using a commercial skirt pattern and instructions, cut out white skirt sections.

Planning the design
The couched designs shown on the skirt on page 60 are made up of simple and straightforward lines; some lines run vertically and parallel (top skirt section), some horizontally and parallel (center section), and the remaining lines intersect to make a diagonal cross-hatched design.

Adapt the couching design to the skirt pattern you have chosen, making changes if necessary. If your plan for stitching is formal, mark the stitching lines on the skirt sections with a water-soluble quiltmaker's pen. For an informal design, marking the stitching lines is unnecessary. Just position the cordings where you desire as you sew.

Couching the design
Set the machine on a narrow (just wide enough to cross over the gold cord), open zigzag stitch.

To couch, lay the gold cord on the stitch line at the raw edge of the skirt section. Bar-tack the end of the cord, and zigzag across the length of the cord, attaching it to the fabric; finish the stitching at the opposite raw edge with bar tacking. Repeat until all gold cords have been attached to all skirt sections.

Assembling the skirt
Following the instructions with the commercial pattern, put skirt together.

Cutwork Blouse

Shown on page 61.

MATERIALS
Purchased blouse or shirt
Rayon sewing thread
Size 11 sewing machine needles
Skein of embroidery floss
Water-soluble transfer pen
Plastic-coated freezer wrap
Typing paper, paper

INSTRUCTIONS
Enlarge pattern, *below,* onto paper. Position the design under the blouse fabric, and trace it onto the blouse with the transfer pen. Slip typing paper under the cutwork motif for stability.

1 Square = 1 Inch

Using a narrow, dense stitch setting, with rayon thread on machine and in bobbin, couch 3 strands of embroidery floss on all transferred lines of pattern.

Cut away shaded areas of design close to, *but not through,* the stitching. Remove all pieces of cutout sections.

Cut freezer wrap to fit under a cutout area and iron to wrong side of fabric (plastic-coated side to fabric). Be careful not to distort the pattern.

Draw lines on freezer wrap with pencil at ¼-inch intervals horizontally and vertically. Set machine for embroidery by removing foot, lowering feed dogs, and setting stitch length and width to 0. *Remember to put foot lever in down position because the lever will affect thread tension even without foot attached.*

Begin stitching over lines behind satin stitching. Take 2 or 3 locking stitches in place, then stitch on top of penciled line, continuing across opening to other side of satin stitching. Stitch over the top of previous stitching and anchor at starting place.

After stitching all lines like this, replace appliqué foot, raise feed dogs, and set machine for a dense ⅛-inch-wide satin stitch. Beginning behind cutwork line, take locking stitches; then stitch over all lines once again.

Restitch original cutwork line with a medium zigzag stitch to enclose line ends, stabilize and smooth cutwork lines. Carefully remove all paper from work.

Do all cutout areas similarly. Flip design and repeat process for other side of garment. Steampress on wrong side to finish.

Pillow Portrait General Instructions

Shown on pages 62–65.

Gathering the materials

Fabrics and trims needed for each pillow are listed with specific directions for individual pillows. In addition, you will need: large sheets of white and tissue paper; ecru, black, and rust embroidery floss; quilt batting; polyester fiberfill; fusible webbing.

Preparing the designs

Enlarge patterns included in specific pillow instructions. Make a copy of enlarged pattern by tracing over original with tissue paper. Do not include embroidered details on tissue paper copy. Save original for reference and cut tissue pattern apart as you progress across the portrait.

Preparing the materials

Begin each portrait by laying a piece of muslin over face on the original drawing. Using a lead pencil, lightly draw in facial features to be embroidered. Also, draw around entire skin shape including neck and shoulders if they are shown in portrait. When cutting out this piece, you need not cut the paper pattern. Cut around penciled shape, adding a ½-inch allowance for turning under when appliquéing to background. Cut another muslin piece exactly the shape of the face without the allowance or penciled-in embroidery lines. This piece lies under first piece and acts as a shadow panel and guide for turning under raw edges of top piece.

Assembling the portraits

Using the original drawing as a guide, pin face pieces in place on background. Embroider facial details, turn, and appliqué raw edges by hand. (Be careful not to pull threads too tightly; this could cause distortion.) Embroider most details with 3 strands of ecru floss. Darken eye pupils with black floss and add a black line over top lid of eye. Satin-stitch the lips.

Once face is established, cut and fuse surrounding costume pieces in place with fusible webbing. Then machine-appliqué with closely spaced zigzag satin stitches.

Begin with head's ear pieces closest to face, work outward and down, cutting one piece (and its webbing) at a time from pattern. Cutting must be precise so that pieces will fit together. You needn't add seam allowances since pieces butt each other.

Finishing the pillows

Add trims, beads, buttons, and feathers by machine or hand. Add velveteen strips around edges of portrait. Lay portrait atop quilt batting, and quilt around portrait shapes, seam lines, and on background lines (see pattern). Cut pillow back to match front. With right sides facing, sew together with ¾-inch seams; leave bottom open. Turn, stuff, and sew closed.

King Henry

Shown on page 62.

Finished size is 21x28 inches.

MATERIALS

¼ yard each of muslin, paisley print, black print broadcloth, black velveteen, rust velveteen, and red satin
22x16-inch piece of gold velvet
22x28½-inch piece of rust velveteen for pillow back
½ yard maroon velveteen
2 yards gold metallic cord
16 inches of ½-inch-wide black lace for shirt trim
⅜ yard 1-inch-wide trim
⅔ yard gold chain trim, large gold button, 12-inch plume
5 inches white lace for collar
Gold, black, and red thread

INSTRUCTIONS

Follow general directions using the pattern, *below*. Sew cording
continued

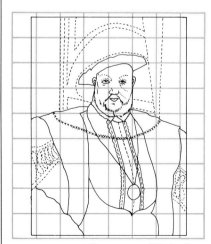

1 Square = 2½ Inches

and black lace in place. Hand-stitch plume, neckwear trim, and necklace in place. Complete pillow front by adding 16x3½-inch maroon velveteen strips at top and bottom and 28½x3½-strips at sides, using 1½-inch seams.

Anne of Cleves

Shown on page 62.

Finished size is 21x26 inches.

MATERIALS
¼ yard muslin
¼ yard pale green chiffon
¼ yard lace fabric
¼ yard gold satin
⅝ yard red velveteen
1 yard red/gold brocade
1 yard ruffled lace trim
1 yard gold velveteen
16x22-inch piece of forest green velveteen
4 green and 1 gold "jewel" buttons set in gold filigree
½ yard gold cord

INSTRUCTIONS
Follow general directions and pattern, *below*. Apply chiffon piece over gold satin and face after they have been stitched. Also, apply a chiffon piece under lace neck overlay. Lace neck can be tucked inside gold satin bodice if a small allowance is added when cutting. Couch gold cording and jewels in place. Work hands and attach over skirt.

1 Square = 2½ Inches

Add 4x16-inch strips of gold velveteen to top and bottom of completed portrait. Add 4x26-inch-long strips to sides.

Catherine of Aragon

Shown on page 63.

Finished size is 16x24 inches.

MATERIALS
⅓ yard muslin
¼ yard black cotton
Scraps of brown-striped cotton, white brocade, and gold satin
17x25-inch piece of gold velvet
¾ yard brown velveteen
½ yard white floral trim
80 inches upholstery cord
⅝ yard black and gold braid
1 yard black/gold tape trim for pillow sides
4 green "jewel" buttons
Black, brown, and white thread

INSTRUCTIONS
Follow general directions and pattern, *below*. For black detail lines on hat, couch 6 strands of embroidery floss with a narrow zigzag machine stitch. Add 5-inch-wide side panels of brown velveteen to completed portrait. Sew decorative tape over side seams. Cover upholstery cording with brown velveteen to make piping. Sew piping around eges of pillow front; back pillow with brown velveteen.

1 Square = 2½ Inches

Anne Boleyn

Shown on page 63.

Finished size is 20x25 inches.

MATERIALS
½ yard muslin
¼ yard brown velveteen
¼ yard gold satin
Scrap of rust velveteen
14x18½-inch piece maroon cotton for background
21x26½-inch piece maroon velvet for pillow back
½ yard maroon velvet for pillow front strips
½ yard black/gold trim
½ yard black lace
½ yard black cotton
⅞ yard pearl trim for necklace
¾ yard gold filigree trim
Black and gold thread

INSTRUCTIONS
Follow general directions and pattern, *below*. Stitch braided trim, lace, and filigree in place. Hand-stitch pearls in place last. Then, add 4½x14-inch strips to top and bottom of portrait and 4½x26½-inch strips to sides.

1 Square = 2½ Inches

Catherine Parr

Shown on page 62.

Finished size is 18x22 inches.

MATERIALS
½ yard muslin
1 yard (40-inch-wide) dark green velveteen
15-inch square red velveteeen
Scraps of red/gold brocade, black velveteen, rust velveteen, white brocade, and white cotton
5 inches of gold trim
12 inches of pearl trim
2 green "jewel" buttons
Peacock feather
Red, black, and white thread

INSTRUCTIONS
Follow general directions and pattern, *below*. Cut a pendant brocade and stitch in place. Stitch gold trim, rings, and feather in place. Attach pearl trim along dotted line on hat. Back pillow with green velveteen.

1 Square = 2½ Inches

Jane Seymour

Shown on page 62.

Finished size is 20x25 inches.

MATERIALS
½ yard muslin
¾ yard blue velveteen
½ yard beige velveteen
Scraps of gold satin, blue brocade, white brocade, black cotton, and paisley print
14 inches gold braid
14 inches pearl trim
2½ yards 1½-inch-wide black/gold trim
Black, gold, and white thread

INSTRUCTIONS
Follow general directions and pattern, *below*. Frame the portrait with 4-inch-wide beige velveteen strips. Use blue velveteen for the pillow back.

1 Square = 2½ Inches

Catherine Howard

Shown on page 63.

Finished size is 20x25 inches.

MATERIALS
¾ yard beige velveteen
½ yard brown velveteen
¼ yard black/gold brocade
20-inch square of black velveteen
Scraps of white brocade, rust cotton, and paisley print
6 inches gold trim
10 inches gold braid, button
Gold, black, and white thread

INSTRUCTIONS
Follow general directions and pattern, *below*. Cut dress trim from black/gold brocade using design indicated by dotted lines on pattern as a guide. After all other costume pieces have been appliquéd, hand-stitch gold trims and ring in place.
To frame portrait, cut two 3¾x20-inch strips from brown velveteen and sew to sides with ½-inch seams. Sew 3x21-inch strips to top and bottom. Use beige velveteen for pillow back.

1 Square = 2½ Inches

"DRAWING AND PAINTING"

ON YOUR MACHINE

Filling your home with favorite family photographs and mementos can create a cozy, personalized mood. The next few pages show you how to capture personal moments of your life in stitchery that will warmly welcome you home.

In a creative spirit of new and adventuresome stitching, here are some bold ideas to try. What you'll find on these and the next few pages will encourage you toward the artistic and toward spending stitching time that is especially meaningful to you and your loved ones.

For example, here's a new twist on an old idea—the album quilt. Shown *at left* are three machine drawings borrowed from family photographs—one from an old group portrait too fragile to remain in the sunlight for long, one from a slide of a precious wedding day, and one from a picture of a present-day home. All of the photographs were made with the simplest of stitches—the straight stitch.

By following the instructions on pages 72 and 73, you can turn your own family photographs into comfortable and familiar accessories for your home.

For still more personalized home accessories, see the rest of this chapter. Included on pages 74–79 are a deck-decorating autograph project and a plan for making your favorite photograph of your child into a permanent fabric portrait.

EXCERPTS FROM THE FAMILY ALBUM

One of the best sources of inspiration for sentimental stitchery is your family album or slide collection. A look through the treasured pages of an album or sets of slides may reveal special moments captured on film that could be taken out, copied in fabric, and enjoyed everyday.

To get started on machine drawings of your own, look through your picture collections for places you've visited, people you've known and loved, and houses you've lived in.

Select pictures that can most successfully be translated into drawings. For example, you'll need large pictures with simple images. Black and white 8x10-inch photographs with high contrasts in light and dark shapes work best; small photographs with complex compositions do not work well. You might also choose formal portraits and professionally photographed scenes. *At left* are samples of the kinds of family pictures that will make successful stitchings.

Before you begin sewing, prepare *reversed* drawings on paper to follow when stitching. Because the stitching is done on the *wrong* side of the materials, a reversed image appears on the *right* side (the bobbin side). Compare the reversed stitching diagram *opposite, lower right* and the picture pillow on page 70.

To prepare paper stitching diagrams of your photographs or slides, choose one of the following methods:

Trace photographs on tissue paper. If you have high-contrast photographs, you'll be able to make tracings of them on tissue paper. To reverse them, draw over the lines on the wrong side of the tissue and photocopy them on sturdier paper.

Trace images from projected slides. Insert slides in the projector in *reverse.* Tape 9x12-inch pieces of paper on the wall in a darkened room and project enlarged images inside the boundaries of the sheets of paper. Focus until you are happy with the composition.

Draw around the images with free-flowing lines that the machine can follow without stopping and starting too often.

Photocopy extra copies, if desired.

Make photocopies of photographs or prints. Libraries, banks, or public buildings have photocopying services for high-contrast photographs. Then, to reverse the prints, tape them to a well-lighted window and trace around the shapes you plan to machine-draw. Or, go to a print shop for additional services such as enlarging, reducing, or reversing.

The materials needed for machine drawing, *upper right,* are simple—muslin, dark thread, fleece padding, and the reversed drawing on paper. Prepare several bobbins of thread so you can sew without interruption.

Practice by stitching on scraps of muslin, fleece, and paper pinned together. Layer them with the muslin on the bottom, fleece in the center and the paper drawing on top. Set your machine on a short straight stitch. Cover or lower the feed dogs and use a darning foot to allow the fabric to move freely under the needle with the presser bar down.

Holding the fabric tautly between the thumb and index finger of each hand, sew along the drawn lines, moving the fabric under the needle to follow the lines. Check the machine tension while stitching. Clip threads often on the front side to prevent catching stray threads. When you feel comfortable with the technique, stitch up your machine drawings. To see how a nearly finished machine drawing looks from the wrong side, see the photograph *at lower right.*

Clip all threads on the front close to the surface to make them presentable, then stitch the completed drawings into pillows, pictures, or book covers.

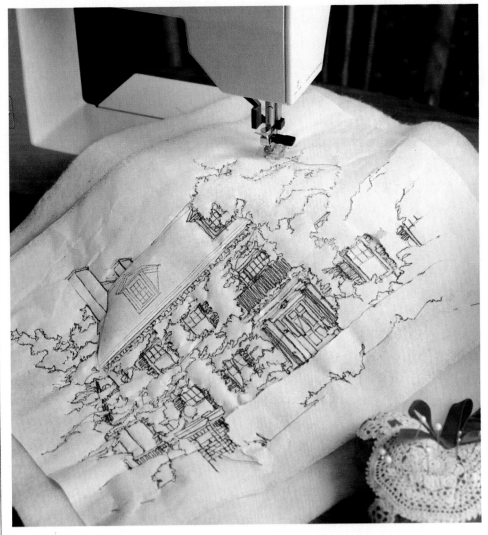

"DRAWING AND PAINTING"

DECORATING WITH AUTOGRAPHS

If you've ever collected autographs, you know the pleasure of owning an intangible treasure, for in the handwritten signatures lies the essence of people you've known and admired.

The butterfly chairs, *left,* are slightly more tangible signs of a unique collection of autographs of friends and relatives. Rejuvenated with colorful new canvas covers for a summer celebration, these classic chairs sport lively line drawings in brilliant satin stitches.

Supply your friends and relatives with a permanent marking pen or laundry marker for signing the canvas. Ask them for *bold* signatures and greetings, as shown *at left.* Then stitch up your collection with wide satin stitches in the brightest of colors.

PAINTING YOUR CHILD'S PORTRAIT WITH FABRIC

The key to "painting" a child's portrait with fabric appliqué is intentional simplicity.

The composition, *right,* is borrowed from the slide photograph shown *opposite, upper left,* and translated into a fresh statement in fabric. A thoughtful limitation of the number of choices in shape, detail, and materials of the original photograph is what makes the portrait pleasant and durable.

To make your own fabric portraits, follow the series of steps outlined below and on the next three pages. Read all of the instructions before beginning.

Choose a slide that will translate easily into fabric appliqué. You will need a composition that gives the figure of the child predominance and that is free from clutter in the background. A portrait-style photograph from the waist up is an easy subject; you'll be able to concentrate on the child's face and upper body. See the photograph *opposite, upper left* for an example of a good subject. Take note of the original details that

do not appear in the finished fabric portrait *opposite.*

Make a line drawing from the slide you have selected. Begin by defining the boundaries of the finished picture; mark it on a large sheet of butcher paper. With masking tape, fasten the paper lightly to a wall in a darkened room.

Using a projector, display the child's photograph onto the paper and adjust the portrait within the defined area. During the adjustment, move the projector back and forth so the child's face is just about life-size and falls as a focal point either to the right or the left above the center of the picture space.

With a fine-pointed marking pen, draw around the projected shapes. As you draw, remember that almost everything you draw will be cut into a fabric shape. *Draw only what you need* to cut out the portrait; do not draw extra details, tiny shapes, and shadows.

Be sure to include face and hair details that can be easily outlined in hand embroidery. See the photograph, *upper right,* for the original line drawing made for the portrait on page 76.

Make a tissue paper cutting pattern. This step is crucial to the final portrait because it is at this point that you plan your design, simplify it again, and determine exactly what shapes to cut from the fabrics and which colors to use.

Trace over the butcher paper drawing (master pattern) on sturdy tissue paper. Ignore superficial detail lines (note the lack of blouse creases and hair outlines in the example, *lower right).* Trace around shapes only, picturing how they can be cut out with scissors. Add facial lines, if desired.

Collect a number of ½-yard lengths of printed and plain fabrics and fabric scraps you think will work in the picture. Include a lightweight skin-toned fabric. Oversupply yourself with choices for the moment and line them up to determine which ones are lightest, light, medium-light, medium, medium-dark, and dark.

Then, use markers in shades corresponding to your fabric collection to fill in the outlined shapes on the tissue drawing, *lower right.* The tissue drawing becomes your color guide and plan for cutting. Eliminate extra fabric choices as you complete your plan.

continued

PAINTING YOUR CHILD'S PORTRAIT WITH FABRIC

With your tissue paper plan completed, you are ready to execute the design. You will need fabrics, fusible webbing, lightweight iron-on interfacing, threads, gray and peach embroidery floss, a water-soluble marking pen, pins, scissors, paper towels, an iron, and a sewing machine.

Prepare the face and hands for embroidery. Place skin-toned fabric over the master drawing; trace around the entire face shape (including ears and neck) with marking pen. Repeat for hand and arm shapes. Draw in all detail lines for embroidery. Fuse iron-on interfacing behind the skin shapes to stabilize them and cut them out ½ inch beyond the outer lines.

Begin the fabric layout by cutting out background fabric with 2-inch stretching margins beyond portrait edges. Place the tissue plan over the background fabric and position the skin shapes behind the tissue; pin as shown, *upper right.* *Note:* Facial embroidery will be done last.

Cut out fabric shapes. Pin the tissue paper plan to the background along the sides and bottom. On the tissue, cut away the background shape already in place. Cut apart a few of the tissue paper head shapes and pin them to various fabrics selected for the hair. Pin fusible webbing behind the fabrics (tissue patterns on top of fabrics) and cut out the three layers without adding seam allowances.

Position the hair sections on the background, fitting the pieces together around the face jigsaw-puzzle style (use remaining tissue plan as a guide). Continue cutting clothing pieces around neck, *center right.*

Fuse the fabrics to the background with an iron when several of the pieces are in position, *lower right.* Place a layer of paper towels between the iron and fabrics to catch stray wisps of the webbing.

Continue the cutting and fusing steps, working toward the bottom of the composition and throwing away the tissue pattern pieces as the fabrics are positioned on the background. *Note:* Be sure to add 2-inch stretching margins to the parts of the shapes that fall along the portrait edges.

When the entire composition is cut and fused, satin-stitch around all raw edges with matching or contrasting threads, *opposite.* Then, staple onto a stretching frame and embroider the remaining details by hand using embroidery floss.

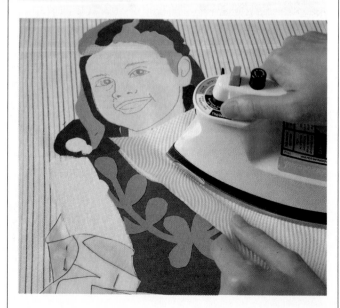

ACKNOWLEDGMENTS

We wish to express our appreciation to the designers, photographers, and others who contributed to this book. When more than one project appears on a page, the acknowledgment specifically cites the project with the page number. A page number alone indicates one designer or source has contributed all of the project material listed for that page.

Our special thanks to the following designers who contributed machine stitchery projects to this book.

Jane Di Teresa—7, tea cozy; 17
Arlette Gosieski—14–15; 16
Verna Holt—18; 19; 20–21; 22
Adam Jerdee—36
Rebecca Jerdee—8; 30–31; 32; 34; 35; 37; 44–45; 48; 60; 62–65; 76–79
Pat Kraus—9
Janet McCaffery—33, doll; 49
Judy Pickett—58
Beverly Rivers—6, shoes
Diane Schultz—70–73
Judith Veeder—4–5; 6–7, sampler pockets; 33, vest; 50–51; 74–75
Jim Williams—47

For their cooperation and courtesy, we extend a special thanks to the following sources of designs and projects.

The New Home Sewing
   Machine Company
171 Commerce Road
Carlstadt, NJ 07072

Pfaff American Sales Corporation
610 Winters Avenue
Paramus, NJ 07652

C.M. Offray & Son, Inc.
261 Madison Avenue
New York, NY 10016

We also are pleased to acknowledge the following photographers, whose talents and technical skills contributed much to this book.

Mike Dieter—6–7, sewing pockets; 18; 19; 20–21; 22; 30–31; 32; 33; 34; 35; 36–37; 50–51, quilt and linens
Hedrich-Blessing—58–59
Hopkins Associates—4–5; 6, shoes; 7, tea cozy; 14–15; 17, how-to photographs; 47, how-to photograph; 48; 49; 50, how-to photographs; 70–71; 72; 73; 74–75; 76; 77; 78; 79
Thomas Hooper—8; 9; 26; 44–45; 46; 30; 62–63; 64; 65
Scott Little—17, embroidered picture, box
Bruce McAllister—16
Perry Struse—47, child's apron

Have BETTER HOMES AND GARDENS® magazine delivered to your door. For information, write to: MR. ROBERT AUSTIN, P.O. BOX 4536, DES MOINES, IA 50336.